995

THE
SUDDENLY
SINGLE
MOTHER'S
SURVIVAL
GUIDE

D0920161

L. Patricia Kite

Mills & Sanderson, Publishers
Bedford, MA • 1991

DISCLAIMER

The author thanks the hundreds of people throughout the United States and Great Britain who, over the past 15 years, have shared their problems, solutions, anecdotes, and adventures. Because many tales of success and woe are common ground for re-entry singles, their stories have been blended to provide the most interest and information. All names used in the text are ficticious.

Published by Mills & Sanderson, Publishers
Box 665, Bedford, MA 01730
Copyright © 1991 L. Patricia Kite

Library of Congress Cataloging-in-Publication Data

Kite, Patricia, 1940-
    The suddenly single mother's survival guide / by Patricia Kite.
      p.   cm.
    ISBN 0-938179-27-6 : $9.95
    1. Single mothers--United States. 2. Single mothers--United States--Life skills guides. I. Title.
HQ759.915.K58   1991   90-25144
306.85'6'0973--dc20   CIP

Printed and manufactured by Capital City Press.
Cover design by Lyrl Ahern and Maria Cronin.
Author photo on back cover by Sally Kite.

Printed and Bound in the United States of America

♦ CONTENTS ♦

To my daughters—

Karen, Laura, Rachel and Sally;

they are the sunrise of my mornings.

Author's Preface

You can't go down for the third time and quietly drown when you're a single parent.

Why not? Because someone is sure to flush, your head will get stuck, and there are few volunteers around to mop up the ensuing flood.

So what can you do? More than you think. I know, because I've been there with four children. At first you see only what seems an endless array of obstacle courses. All the advice you're getting seems tinged with doomsday predictions. Your confidence level is already well below zero, and it's rapidly sinking. You have been removed from Cinderella's castle, and placed, seemingly forever, among the ashes.

The future seems positively dismal. Maybe it would, after all, be better if somebody flushed, even if it did leave a mess. After all, you're never going to smile again ... or so you think.

It Can Only Get Better

Actually you will smile, grin, giggle, chuckle and laugh. You will even tell jokes, corny or otherwise. Long ago, a *been-through-it* person told me that there's no place to go from the bottom, but up. It's true. You may have been ejected from a dream world into reality, but reality has multiple dimensions, one of which is having fun.

That's what this book is about. How to gain a practical *re-entry* life brushed with a touch of humor.

Why This Book Was Written

When I first joined the ranks of solo parents, I went to the library seeking tomes to help me dog paddle. There were books on widowhood, how to keep a disastrous marriage together, psychological diatribes on kids from broken homes, multiple editions on how a svelte 25-year-old could effectively conquer the single's scene, primers with miniscule print telling me everything best learned from a lawyer and/or the welfare department, plus large-print texts with glossy photographs on how to cook Crepes Suzettes for 1½ persons. So I muddled along unaided, and every time a spasm particular to re-entry shook my already shaken body I figured, "You are the only one this has ever happened to."

It was several years after my emergence as a *single-again* parent that I discovered I wasn't "the only one," but one among many who had similar experiences. Why didn't anybody tell me this at starting point, when I really needed the help?

I thought about this book for years before finally writing it. Discussing the concept with single and single-again friends, they kept saying "Don't forget to mention this ..." and "Don't forget to mention that ...." It would take a multiple-volume encyclopedia to cover all the things people told me to mention.

Many items are best left to lawyers, physicians, and spiritual counselors. I do not pretend to be any of these. My credits include raising four sane, relatively sensible, and competent children. The youngest of whom was 4 months old when I filed for divorce.

In my subsequent work as a hospital rehabilitation supervisor, and later as a professional writer, I met many wonderful people who shared their thoughts and coping methods. To these people, and to my married and solo friends, I say thank you. Without their support and continual nagging to "Write it, don't just talk about it," I would have spent long evening hours daydreaming about a book instead of getting it done.

I hope, as you read, you smile, find companionship, and learn coping techniques. Among the many practical suggestions here, you may find a few that seem somewhat zany. But these methods worked for me and they might work for you.

Good luck.

GETTING THROUGH
THE FIRST DAY

There's an organization that regularly takes sleek suburban and city-bred youngsters, arms them with a couple of asparagus spears and some parsley, then deposits them in the middle of the wilderness to survive among wolves, bears and assorted snakes.

At the close of x number of days, the youngsters are supposed to emerge apple-cheeked, bursting with vigor, and forever psychologically armed with the knowledge they have tackled the unknown and won, hands down.

For this knowledge, their parents pay a great deal of money. Congratulations! You are now getting the same experience, free of charge!

Whether you have held an outside job, or devoted your energies to the domestic hearth, the day hubby trots out the door with an embarrassed wave of his goodbye hand, you have just been cannon shot into wilderness; nor do you have a parachute to ease the landing.

Along with the parsley in the cupboard and the wilted asparagus in the refrigerator, there's a bit of extra baggage in your knapsack. To be precise, you have children of assorted shapes and sizes who are also listening as those last echoes of a fire-engine red Porche fade into the distance.

1

Silence will last exactly five seconds. After this, the children turn and stare at you, a dull gleem of expectation in their sad, scared little eyes.

From someplace within your battered psyche, you must muster the strength to square back your shoulders, take a deep breathe, smile, and summoning every ounce of confidence in your voice say briskly, "There, there, now. Everything's going to be all right."

If it sounds like the last thing in the world you want to say, it is. While the funeral mechanisms are different, divorce may easily be compared to the death of a loved one. And anybody who thinks you should be other than sad is putting you on, or has lost touch with reality.

Certainly you're glad to get rid of Herman or Harry who made the last few years of your life a living hell. No more will your days resemble a world welterweight championship match, nor your marital chats a hog-calling contest. But that doesn't mean you're happy. It just means you can breathe a sigh of relief without the customarily snide remarks.

However, limit yourself to one deep sigh. The children are still staring at you, remember? How could you forget? Somehow you have to figure out what to do with that first hour after Daddy departs.

Solution: don't do anything. Get into bed; if younger offspring want to cuddle in bed with you, that's fine too. There's nothing like warm bodies when you're feeling like the whole world just deserted you. Stay in bed. Drink hot tea. Watch television reruns. Eat chocolate with the kids; the roof could blow off the house, but if children have chocolate, they feel better. You can cry if you want to. By the time I got around to getting a divorce, I was so cried out it took years for me to work up any new tears.

On the other hand, if hysterics make you feel better, by all means, enjoy them. If you have trouble getting the first hot tears to fall, think of your long dead hamster, or other beloved childhood pet. Think of how you felt when that fuzzy friend passed away in your arms. Think of the afternoon you held the funeral.

If that doesn't work, eat three more nut-enriched chocolates and get on the scale. This will surely make you cry. During this period, it is economically sound to use, instead of neatly packaged tissues, a roll of toilet paper for your droobly nose. Toilet paper is symbolic at this point for how you feel about yourself anyhow.

Adding to your misery, if it's at all possible, is the sight of one or more of your children starting to cry. Don't waste your time on a guilt trip; share your toilet paper, instead. The children need a catharsis just as much as you do. It speeds the healing.

Eventually, just when you begin to feel you have sprouted roots into your mattress, and that staying under the warm bedcovers forever is a splendid idea, nature will issue an urgent summons, calling you out, however temporarily, of your fetus-curled position.

The sight of Mommy stumbling swollen-eyed toward the potty usually reminds the children that they haven't eaten anything but chocolates all day. "We're hungry," they chime. You may be tempted to point yourself toward the kitchen and stir up a burnt offering. But this isn't necessary. You do not have the energy to stand over a stove mushing spaghetti. It's possible you are one of those super efficient people who always has something in stock for every emergency, or you may have some TV dinners or pot pies that will quiet the hunger pains. However, if nothing like this is available, dial the local pizzaria and have them deliver an "everything on it," giant size. This gives the children something to anticipate, since pizza, like chocolate, soothes all wounds.

An alternative, if you cannot muster the strength to dial the phone, is placing a jar of peanut butter, a jar of jam, a spoon, and a loaf of bread on the kitchen table. Place a pile of napkins adjacent to this. Then let the youngsters go to it. Peanut butter is very soothing.

All this may sound like you're starting your new journey down the road to ruin, but actually you're lightening your load by discarding trite old standards that will bog you down on your road to success. And the first BIG WORD you must junk is SUPPOSED. Supposed to eat broccoli with each meal. Supposed to have a shining floor. Supposed to press the bed linens. Supposed to volunteer at the school. Supposed to be a "good little girl."

I spelled masochism with a capital M for years, just doing all the dribs and drabs of things that some person long ago told me I was *supposed* to do. Then, I removed the word from my vocabulary, shredded it up, and filed it under "t" for "toilet." It was the first step toward escaping the wilderness in which I felt trapped.

And so you take each day ... one step at a time. And eventually you will scale that mountain that lays before you, and glory in the wonder of the view from the top.

What About the Second Day?

There will be a marked temptation to tackle everything at once, doing it all between crying jags. You find yourself immediately wanting to move from your present residence, at the same time starting a job search, finding a husband, locating a devoted boyfriend, plus getting your offsping back on the straight and narrow. You flutter around in a whirlwind of often aimless activity, wondering why the world isn't conforming to neat and orderly expectations.

Best advice: "Tackle first things first." Set your priorities and stick to them.

Although your goals may be different, my first priority was getting the kids calmed down. I figured if they continued to be upset, I would continue to be upset. I wanted ... needed ... a stable home life, something that hadn't been around for quite a while. So all my efforts were focused in that direction.

My efforts paid off, although it took much longer than I expected. There are a variety of behavior patterns that emerge after a divorce just due to the chaos that tend to exist beforehand. Most of the behaviors are short term, but others will interminably drive you up the wall. When the patterns seem more than you can handle, though you are trying as hard as you can, don't be afraid to seek professional help. It is available, often at lower cost than you think. Many local city-funded counseling centers exist. A few sessions with a trained impartial advisor not only helps the *problem* child, but his mother as well.

Forget the moving idea. Put it off as long as possible. Dump the idea all together if you can. First, your children have been through enough disruption. You don't want to drag them through any more changes than you have to. Second, take a hard look at those old memories. What's really, truly bothering you about your current home?

I was ready to transport my children cross-country, putting my tacky furniture on my back if I had to. Fortunately common sense and a moving estimate made me look for alternatives. What was in the house that bothered me so much? Every mental picture focused on the bed. That's right, the bed. The king-size expensive orthopedic contraption which brought daily and nightly recollections of connubial snuggling. So I put an ad in the local newspaper and sold the galumpher. Then I went out and purchased a very reasonably priced double bed. There was less room to thrash around in by myself, but it still afforded enough space for a lonesome youngster or two. Relief was instantaneous. My castle suddenly looked brighter and *all mine.*

If purchasing a new bed is financially out of question, dig into the budget and get new sheets. Replace masculine plaid with feminine floral, trade in blues and greens for vibrant pinks and purples. Sheets can be almost dirt cheap when you buy them on sale, and they last practically forever. You'll be surprised at the difference they make in your attitude, and wonder why you didn't think to make the switch even sooner. Use your old linens for dustcloths, or better yet give them to a worthwhile charity. Maybe this will help some other *suddenly single* person who also wants to change bed coverings.

A friend, who planned on selling her low-monthly-payment house and purchasing another with an exorbitant second mortgage, took my advice on this subject. Afterwards she gave me a big hug and said, "Not only is *that* idea a lifesaver, but you also might mention a new bedspread." I immediately purchased a red, white and blue quilt to replace my *reminder* brown velvet spread. Eventually I got new dishes, too. Meal time or slumber time, images of marriages past were no longer present with every fork clank or tucking of the bed spread.

When your mental peace seems a bit more assured, then you can go job hunting. If you have to do this immediately for severe financial reasons, find a position with the lightest psychological load and the most regular work hours. It may pay a little less, or a lot less, but if you obtain a high pressure, erratic overtime form of employment, you'll have even less time for getting your family and your life together.

Eventually everything will pile up on you, like a multi-car collision on a fog-enshrouded speedway, and the job won't hold anyhow. So start slow and figure on career climbing at a slightly later date.

Last, but not least, the male replacement. No stalwart with brains above the ankle-socks line is going to take on a host of characters right out of looney tunes. Should you place *replacement male* high on your hit list, you'll certainly corral someone who needs a leaning post, a con artist, or a dude who insists on helping you, while at the same time insisting you stay helpless.

In very recent memory you've done the Him-Twaddle-You-Tush routine. Unless you really miss that self-effacing set up, give your wounds a chance to heal in peace. Mental strength attracts mental strength; Stalwart Fellow will turn up, should you still want him, when common sense and clearer vision allows you to differentiate the mighty oak from the dandelion.

Set realistic priorities and you will come out well ahead of the game. I've had gentlemen propose, not despite my kids, but because they "really like" my kids. It's difficult, they say, to find a single parent with a "really stable family life." Now that's a compliment well worth waiting for. You will hear it too, after panic bells have muted into dulcet tones. Harmony, not cacophony, is what you're after. So take re-entry procedures one note at a time.

LADY FRIENDS AND FIENDS

Umpteen million doomsayers will tell you that all your *comes-in-pairs* friends will desert you en masse the day your divorce papers hit the county recorder's file box. This isn't true. Some will, of course, vanish instantaneously. Others will stick around temporarily. A third group will remain permanent fixtures, providing a fantastic support system. There's no fortune teller's way of predicting who's who, but there are a few clues to help take the edge off the present shock.

Typhoon Marys

Women connected with hubby's business, even though you attended many mutual cocktail parties, at your home and theirs, will almost automatically clock out of your social scene.

This can lead to a bit of ultra-cynicism as you wonder why you ever bothered associating with these jerks in the first place. You could have better spent the time, perhaps, doing aerobics at the health club—or even dusting. But there is no use getting uptight about their vanishing act. You would have lost contact with these women if you moved out of town, if your husband switched jobs, or if their husband switched jobs.

7

Looking at it from a practical perspective, you won't put *Typhoon Mary* on your hit list. Besides, you can never tell, if the vanishing lady herself emerges on the suddenly single scene, as happens often enough these days, you might just renew your acquaintance; you will now have something in common again.

As a side note, this can prove to be great fun. In addition to a new-found sympathy for your miseries, you will also get to trading juicy tidbits of gossip that neither of you would mention while both were married. Keep this in mind before building a grudge. Times change, and people change with them.

Another instant disappearing act, although they were never truly present in the first place, are those whom I term "casual environmental acquaintances." You've shared occasional coffees, perhaps chatted about kids and domestic duties, or maybe even shared stapling three-part flyers for committees, fund raisers, and lady's aid societies. Along comes your divorce, and somehow the coffee pot short circuits and the committee chairwoman, who "didn't know how she would ever get along without you," manages to lose your phone number. All this when you now have ample time and would actually welcome a group stapling or envelope licking party.

For example, two days after my divorce, when I certainly didn't need any additional ice picks, a neighborhood person made it a point of stopping me on the street. "Horace and I are extremely happy together," she said distinctly. "He is the best thing that ever happened to me, and we really get along well." In addition to this, she intended to work hard to preserve her connubial bliss, and hoped there "wouldn't be any interference." This closed the conversation. Her meaning, quite clear, was I "shouldn't even breathe in the direction of her spouse." I hadn't even thought about her spouse, and wouldn't have even if he was served up with an apple in his mouth. And you can be sure there are a few women like this in your immediate or not too far-flung vicinity.

You may, if you choose, surreptitiously glare at these rude souls with your laser-beam third eye, and let it go at that. Or you can mumble, "Wait until it's your turn, lady," figuring statistics will at least make her a widow, and then she'll know how it feels. But, in time, as your own life horizons expand and Mrs. Insulated's continue to be surrounded by no-see-through plasticine walls, you come to feel more pity than censure. Also, in time, you become your own person in the community, and a respected person at that. In which case, most drop their shiver and shake routine and sometimes actually start feeling quite envious. In fact, they may cross the street, as my neighborhood person did, and say, "How are you? Haven't seen you around lately."

Depending on your mood, you smile serenely or casually inquire whether her spectacles have been misplaced for the last few years. In some instances, she will coerce you into a *just-like-past-life* cup of coffee. If you acquiesce, you will soon wonder what you ever talked about, eons ago. You have changed-changed-changed, she hasn't. There is nothing that makes you realize how far you've come than trying to pick up the threads of a threadbare, long ago relationship. But you do walk away from Mrs. Insulated taking a breath of fresh air, and with an extra lilt to your step. It's something to look forward to, in its own crazy way.

Temporary Tillies

Immediately, and for approximately one year after your venture into singledom, you will receive a plethora of telephone calls from Mrs. Concern, Mrs. Solicitious, and Mrs. Interested-in-Your-Well-Being. Most of these calls start out with some variation of, "Oh, you poor dear. I've been so worried about you. How are things going over there now that hubby has left you all alone to raise those sweet, defenseless children?"

The inquirer waits, not maliciously, not consciously, to hear of the latest misery that has befallen your hapless brood now that it is without a supreme male being. She cluck-clucks. She encourages you to tell all the current gory details. She'd also like you to amplify any past gory details that you might have inadvertently omitted in previous conversations.

What will you do? Glad for a sympathetic ear, you will start spouting like Mount Vesuvius, sniping at your former spouse, listing every facet of his impeccably awful behavior, reviewing and renewing any real or imagined insult that has bruised your ego since the day you innocently said, "I do."

Dumping on your ex-spouse is like a good enema when you're constipated. It gives a welcome sense of relief to point out to

everybody in particular, and anybody in general, how that unap-
preciative trout has treated someone as pure of soul as yourself.
It's very important that all and sundry know your side of the story,
since the person you're talking to might bump into ex-spouse at
the garbage dump and hear his side of the tale first. (I know he
doesn't seem to have a side of the tale, but he might think so.)
Sometimes you will hear yourself repeating the same travails over
and over, forgetting what you already told to whom. But still you
can't control your word flow, at least not for a while.

One day you will truly hear yourself. You will hang up the
phone receiver and think, "How dull. Surely I've got something
else to discuss;" like my co-workers, my boss, my current night
school class, the foibles of politicians, the criminal justice system,
the plumbing, anything. And so you gradually stop the minute
dissection of your former spouse's eccentricities. And it will follow,
like the day follows the night, that Temporary Tillie will also very
gradually stop her telephone calls. She now has nothing for the
gossip circuit, nothing to spice up her life, nothing to make her feel
happy she isn't you.

Temporary Tillie will move on to other poor soul, with her
"Oh, you poor dear," and renew that cycle so necessary for her
existence. This really is okay, because while you will miss Temporary Tillie, you won't miss her all that much. However you can wave
farewell with a friendly handkerchief, for she served a valuable
purpose. Buddies are sometimes buddies because you need them
at the time. Not all good folk will willingly listen to a one-sided
recitative of your woes, so silently give thanks to Tillie, even though
you have moved on to more constructive conversation.

Goodfolks

Another group of temporary Tillie-like friends who should be
mentioned are what I call *his and hers*. They are married folk who
have, perhaps for many years, enjoyed social innings and outings
with you and your spouse. You would discuss trends of the day with
the lady and your spouse would discuss who-hit-what-home-run
with the gentleman.

The Goodfolks are actually friends to both of you, and not of the category where you are chums with the wife, and your hubby comes along for companionship, or vice-versa. And *there* is precisely where the problem lies, for the Goodfolks will have to decide which adult in your family they wish to keep.

Initially, not wanting to take sides, they may try to juggle both of you, inviting ex-hubby on second and fourth Fridays, and you on first and third Fridays, or something similar. This sounds like a great idea, but in practice it is impractical.

One, since it is so typical in the first few years following a divorce for ex-spouses to slander each other as part of the general conversation, an endeared listener often has difficulty coping with the information received, and yet doesn't know how to tune out without appearing totally unsympathetic.

Two, the listeners may find themselves, inadvertently or with all good intentions, passing on information to the opposing ex-spouse. I.e., "Ernestine says she really, truly cares for you, despite all that has happened." (That's not true at all, but you had too many piña coladas that evening. You just got a bit maudlin over the sherry. However, this starts a ruckus; especially if you're the one who initiated the divorce. Another tidbit that commonly starts trouble when inadvertently communicated is "Ernest says he's got this super new side job that pays really well." (Ernest has neglected to mention this to you, and you rush off to your attorney in an attempt to raise alimony/child support payments.)

Three, the Goodfolks are having a super-duper Christmas, New Year's, or other holiday party. You would truly like to attend. However, the party is being held on Ernest's second visiting Friday rather than your third visiting Friday. So they invite Ernest rather than you. You find out about it; you sulk. You can't do anything about this, which makes it worse. It just isn't polite to complain about not receiving invitations to a private festivity. So instead, you nurse a grudge, which erodes away at your relationship with the Goodfolks.

The Goodfolks are in a no-win situation. Eventually they may begin to pull away from one of you, gradually. They may claim, for instance, "You live such a toll call away." More often, you will pull away from them. You want them to choose between the two of you, and when they won't you bow out to avoid the emotional energy drain associated with playing *friendship ping-pong.*

Your split from the Goodfolks won't come right away, but as your post-divorce circle of friendships widens, you will be making choices as to who to keep and who to discard. And, there are only so many hours in the day or week for socializing. You may not even realize that your friendship with the Goodfolks has dropped to practically nothing until you stop and think, "Gosh, I haven't seen Gloria in six months." But you still don't pick up the telephone and call. It is a pity, since they are both nice people, but sharing them is too difficult, so you opt out—and thus they fall into the *temporary* category.

Permanent Pauline

By now you may be wondering what has happened to the friends you were supposed to keep; the true, blue, forever friends. They are there, often friends of *yours* who seldom, if ever, came in contact with hubby. They may also be part of a couple with whom you regularly couple-socialized, but your husband was more of a backdrop than genuine participant. Ernest was invited because he was your spouse, however he never did have much in common with Paul or Pauline. So the relationship continues as if hubby never existed, which he practically didn't as far as this friendship goes.

The Permanent Paulines of this world tend to have extremely solid marriages, but that fact won't prevent an initial suspicion of your intentions. This is the hurdle you must overcome if you want to keep this nice lady as part of your valuable emotional support system. Practically everyone is afraid of a new divorcee in the immediate throes of being suddenly-single. Stories abound of how not-so-defenseless Dolly pounced on defenseless Paul while unsuspecting Pauline was visiting her mother, having boils removed, going to cooking school, etc. And, since a good man is hard to find, no happily attached female is going to welcome a potential competitor into her home, or turn her back for a moment. To overcome instinctive jitters, you've got to work within a carefully constructed game plan.

For example, you have no doubt heard, over and over again, that you should keep your "grubby little paws" off anybody else's husband. This is an oversimplification. You must not only keep your paws off, but also knees, elbows, boobs, belly button and breath. To put it in less physical terms, unless you make every effort to convince a married woman that you have no interest in, and no need for, her hubby's services, you will not be able to continue a relationship of any kind with her.

How do you prove that you're not a potential competitor, given the fact that you don't want Paul—even wrapped in pretty paper and tied with a bow! Basically, you've got to avoid him like the plague for at least a year. It's not enough to keep away from him, the game plan says you even time your visits to Pauline so that they concur with Paul's absences. Even when you do this, you may occasionally find him arriving home unexpectedly. If this happens, finish that cup of coffee within 10 seconds, make the briefest of courteous greetings, grab your coat and purse, and make for the door. Nothing will persuade you to stay. Do not accept a ride home. Do not accept an offer of help with your groceries. Do not remember to ask whether Pauline's pooch has gotten rid of its roundworms. Just go, and give Pauline a friendly follow-up call in a few days.

Never, under any circumstances, call Paul as you might have done in your safely married past and ask him to help fix a fuse, plumbing fixture, or flat tire. That type of helping hand, now that you are single, is strictly off limits. If you can't afford an electrician, plumber or auto mechanic, then go to night school and learn how to do handy-work yourself.

It also doesn't hurt, when socializing with Pauline, to avoid dressing in your favorite slinky, low-cut, or frilly social-scene-dress. If you are up to it, wear curlers, forget makeup, let your stomach hang out a bit, and put on sneakers. It's not enough to avoid being direct competition, you must not look the part either. There will be time enough for the dressing up when you are out making the social scene on your own or with a new beau. Pauline won't be impressed by your beauty, especially if it's new found because you are trying to keep your ego up, or just trying harder. She likes you for your plain ordinary self, and if Paul meanders in and catches you looking a lot plainer than she does, all the better.

You will also need to monitor your conversation as part of this new game plan. The safest topics are your kids, the price of food, your newest decorating scheme, your job, or the shenanigans of the local school board or town council. It is also within acceptable boundaries to chat about your former spouse and his foibles, since you are going to do this anyhow. Good friend Pauline doesn't mind providing a comforting ear, but courtesy and common sense demand that you don't over do it. When you find her gaze wandering toward the wall clock, it's time to move on.

Do not be tempted to liven up the atmosphere by presenting your single social life in glorified exaggeration, such as proclaiming that "sex is absolutely marvelous with Zeus." You can mention that you are attending single's functions, thereby subtly pointing out a lack of interest in entering the married-man market. You can mention, keeping erotic details to a minimum and amusing anecdotes to a maximum, the fellow you dated last week. You can mention how difficult re-entering this type of world is for you, given your long-term adjustment to marriage. It should be made very clear to stably-married Pauline that you are a woman devoted to home and hearth, just like she is. Even though you are now solo, and it's much harder to raise your children properly, you are working toward this end. In fact, it is your primary interest in life.

If you have your head on straight, this is probably the truth. If you're still getting your act together, lie. In this situation, gilding the lily a bit is a definite personality plus.

All this may seem like the most ridiculous advice. After all, the single's world is your life now. Just as Pauline mentions Paul every once in a while, you want to talk about what's realistically going on in your life. But Pauline, wedded since high school or college days, is no more likely to understand the world you are talking about than you understood it during your years of marital bliss. Even worse, Pauline is liable to misunderstand what you are talking about.

For example, you met three absolutely great guys at Big Apricot's single's ski club. You managed to charm each of them so much that a fight ensued over who would get your accurate phone number. It was a great evening, and a group of you went bar hopping afterward. Then you went to somebody's house, where several lively folk enjoyed the hot tub together, etc.

Such outings will occur in your new life with varying frequency, depending on your tastes in companionship. However, from the standpoint of a long-time married woman, the translation may be, "Prudence's lifestyle has certainly changed. She's turning into a regular floozy. Better watch out…" Your married women friends may listen, but it does give them a case of the jitters.

As a single woman, you and Pauline can no longer relate as mutual wives. However, you can continue to relate to her as mother-same and friend-same. This commonality acts as a bonding agent.

For a really tight bond with Permanent Pauline, endear yourself forever by taking her kids along when going to the zoo, park, or roller-skating rink. I hauled so many kids around my first divorced year that I felt like I was running a combination nursery school and day care center. But when it began to feel like *too* much, I reminded myself that everybody likes people who appreciate their children. Also, everybody thrives on having some free time when the little ones are off being properly chaperoned for the day. In addition, you are helping your children hold on to their friendships. They need a stable lifestyle as much as you do.

These tactics can work very well indeed. I kept every one of my married woman friends that I chose to keep. Not only did they lose their initial reservations, but after a year or so had passed they even offered their husbands' services as plumber, electrician, business advisor and mechanic. I continued to be invited to couples-mostly parties, where I continued obeying common sense conversation and action rules, lest other guests take fright. I also became the person many friends called on to help sister Sally or cousin Cora when they were forced into the single's scene. This is, to me, the ultimate compliment.

But I still have to keep on my toes. For example, a married woman-friend at work invited me to a Christmas party. I looked forward to attending, dressed nicely but conservatively, brought along a bottle of wine like a good guest, and entered into the group spirit of conversation. All went well until later in the evening when I got to talking with the hostess' husband. We happened to share a common interest in photography, and he offered to show me his latest tripod. To me it was all business, and the tripod was in his study, which seemed safe enough.

In the study, we started chatting about camera equipment. Very interesting. Can you guess who walked in and saw us engaged in animated conversation alone in the study? You're right. Wifey immediately dragged hubby off to "pour some champagne," even though I don't think they were serving any, and she was distinctly cool toward me at work after that. And I hadn't done anything but talk about macro lenses.

Innocent on my part, but also stupid. We need the Permanent Pauline's in our life. Not only for the emotional support they offer and the homestyle social life they provide, but for their access to single men upon whom they often turn match-making capabilities. It is best not to offend or turn off such kindnesses, any which way you can avoid doing so.

Single Sally

Joining the Permanent Paulines of your friendship circle will eventually be the Single Sallys, otherwise known as divorced or never-married women. How quickly you meet these single's-scene cohorts depends on how aggressively you cast your net. Appearances to the contrary, single women just don't enter your life spontaneously. You have to seek them out.

One way of meeting other singles is to become an active, rather than passive, member of a single's oriented group. Try joining a committee, helping plan parties, or assisting in stapling the newsletter. All these activities require sporadic small group meetings where the same people get together to share coffee, crumpets, and labor. Chances are you'll find at least one individual whose personality jibes with yours. This will help beat the lonelies when you just want to chat, take time off from mothering, go to a movie, or take an evening excursion to the local shopping mall.

Another way of meeting single folk is going back to school. Women, in record numbers and of all ages, are returning to campus life. They may be there to earn a degree, augment knowledge, or improve skills. The catalyst for many of these re-entry students is free time because they are single. The chances are good that the people who chose the same classes you did will also share some common interests with you. Whether community college or university or evening school, you have ample time in a very protected atmosphere, to share study and other common interests and to get to know each other.

Going back to school not only perks up your thinking processes, it also perks up your social life. This is especially true if you are as fortunate as I was in meeting super-nice people who give super-great parties, where you get to meet other interesting people —including men.

Never say you don't have the time. That used to be my argument, accompanied by a recitative of my job commute, job hours, mothering obligations, and house cleaning backpile. Then one evening, after a breakup with my then-current beau, I started listing the dismal time I had spent in pouting, grousing, and pillow punching. I figured that I had spent two hours each day for two weeks on "lonesome me" grumps. All that added up to fourteen hours each week in wasted time. Surely it could be better used elsewhere, such as in an effort to earn a college degree.

I attended night classes for three years—despite a full work week, four kids, and at one time a very ill and dying father. Many of the people in my graduating class were the ones with more responsibilities, rather than those with less. We were more highly motivated.

Advanced education means not only new friends and expanded horizons, but greater job opportunities and promotions. And it really takes only a few hours of your spare time. If you doubt you have any spare time, keep track of the hours you spend watching television, talking on the telephone about how busy you are, and going on shopping trips. That is spare time, and it doesn't even include card playing, single's bars and dating fellows you don't like just to go out.

If tuition money creates a roadblock toward more education, there are many re-entry scholarships available, some even begging for applicants. Talk to several counselors at several schools. Don't limit your investigations to one person. Each counselor will tell you something different, and you will learn the rules as you go. Then apply for scholarships and grants and loans, even if you think you don't have a chance.

For example, after much scurrying around being told I was ineligible for aid because I owned a home, I was tempted to throw in the towel. Then I got a telephone call from a counselor I hadn't met, but who had found my application in the school office files. One particular scholarship I was qualified for had surfaced, was I interested? What did I have to lose?

I spent eons over endless forms, filling in every blank, getting recommendations, rushing to meet the deadline, all the while figuring I didn't have a chance. A month passed and I didn't hear anything. I forgot about it. Then I got a phone call.

I was among three finalists out of 49 hopefuls. And it wasn't because of my grade-point average either. Apparently 24 of the potential applicants didn't like filling out the endless forms, so they didn't bother to return them. Another ten applicants didn't fill out the forms the correct way, so they were disqualified. Seven more applicants didn't make the effort to scrounge up recommendations, so they were also disqualified. Only eight managed to complete the whole package, except five sent it in after deadline, which was too late.

Come interview day, there were three people still in the running, and one didn't show up. That left two of us. We both spoke so earnestly that the scholarship was split two ways.

A third method of acquiring single friends is joining a professional organization. There is one for almost every type of trade, business, skill, goal or hobby. However you can't just pay your dues and expect organization members to rush to your side offering instant friendship.

You must put out that little bit of extra effort. Consider chairing a committee. If you don't like to chair committees, look for one that won't take much time or effort. This enables you to see the same small group over and over again, rather than dealing with large gatherings of unknowns.

Offer to pick people up, or share a ride to the meetings. This gives you a chance for an even more comfortable chat, as well as saving on gas costs. Offer to make telephone calls nobody else wants to make. Save these up for an evening when you're feeling horribly lonesome and desperately in need of a live voice to talk to about anything, even the weather. After you have talked with ten people, any two of whom may be in as much need of conversation as you are, you will have not only done a good deed but you'll feel a lot better too.

After taking the time to visit several organizations, you will find people who suit your needs and interests. Don't hesitate to switch groups if the one you have chosen ends up offering no friendlies. Some organizations are unfortunately quite cliquey. Others are made up of people who like to debate a bit too much, lean toward snobbery, or indulge in advanced back-biting.

Hunt around for a group that doesn't make you feel like a permanent outsider. Then jump in with both feet and become an insider. It's not only fun, but since you are in a professional or trade organization, you are also on the fastest track toward finding out where the better paying job opportunities are, when they're about to happen, and how you can get there first.

Your single friends offer facets which your married friends cannot offer. For example, they tend to be much more *au courant* as to what's going on out there on the social scene. If you want to talk about that evening at the ski lodge, you can be blunt, not blunted. Single friends are also more likely to be available to go out to dinner on a Saturday night, to a play, or for a family hiking afternoon. When you call, spur of the moment, and say "how about dropping everything and coming over for a glass of wine or cup of coffee," single's don't have to dump hubby to get out for a few hours.

It's nice to be able to pick and choose, depending on your mood and time frame, the type of person from your expanding friendship circle who best meets your immediate needs. You have lost some buddies with your entrance into the solo world. Your ability to fill that void augments your ability to survive while smiling.

You, even though perhaps shy, will find the procedure easier than expected. You will not have to cope with husbandly commentary on your choice of acquaintances, his time schedule, his demands that you stay home and hold his hand, even though that hand—like the rest of his body—is snoring in front of the television set.

Pick up the daily newspaper. Look through the section that lists town meetings and organizational dinners, and then go. These notices are not put in the paper just to occupy space; these groups really want you.

So get involved with that single's group, call your local junior college or university and request a class catalogue, and join that professional organization. It sets a good example for your children, in addition to doing something for yourself. Mother is doing something constructive with her life. People are talking to her as if she's a real human being rather than a casualty unit.

Children feel better when they see you taking constructive action. It proves all is not so rocky in their little world, and this is nice to know.

MARRIED MEN AND OTHER MOSQUITOES

Good news! Ten percent of your girlfriends' husbands, and assorted other married-male social acquaintances, will not proposition you after your divorce. Just the knowledge that these dedicated diamonds exist gives hope that a similar single stalwart can be part of your future.

Not so good news. No matter how fleet of foot you are, or how circumspect, you will eventually receive sundry invitations by the remaining 90 percent.

But don't become too cynical, or too hysterical, when Mr. Just-Celebrated-His-25th-Anniversary tries to pat your fanny, or suggests you meet him to watch the sun come up, or go down, at the nearest parking lot.

Remember: Men often think they are expected to make a pass at a newly divorced woman. Their machismo is therefore at stake. If you handle it properly, they will not only be forever grateful you have turned them down, but they will also have increased respect for you.

Translation: Most married men would probably die of fright if you took them up on their invitations, and there's no need to make the male/female ratio in your age bracket even worse.

So how do you handle these not-too-delightful situations? Whether he uses a soft whisper or the clutch and grab routine, keep in mind that a sense of humor is often just as effective as a skunk bomb, and the stink goes away faster. This is especially true when your admirer is a neighbor or other local that you will have to keep greeting at the supermarket or community center baseball games.

The Octopus Fingers shtick usually takes place at a party, where a few ounces of aged rot-gut releases even the best of male safety catches. Your immediate reaction, which you may want to rehearse at home, should be a hearty laugh! This throws the offender off balance. He doesn't know if you're chortling at his abortive techniques, which probably haven't been utilized since he was a skinny teenager, or you actually think the whole attempt is a big joke.

Octopus Fingers will want to believe the latter. Follow-up the advantage gained by this ego-saving move by remaining stiff as a board and speaking LOUDLY. Your volume is very important. The last thing hubby wants is for wifey, or some other spy, to find out what he is up to.

So you say, "Oh, Ethelrod Octopus, you are just the biggest joker, HA-HA-HA. But please be careful where you put your hands, as I have this VERY BAD BACK. In fact, just the other day, the chiropractor told me that I had the worst VARICOSE VEINS he had ever seen, plus my UTERINE POLYPS are enormous, and this continual MUCUS drip in my throat might require the services of a specialist."

Should Ethelrod still be hanging on, don't forget to mention your HEMHORROIDS, plus the BLADDER that lets loose whenever you sneeze.

None of what you say has to particularly make any sense. Just keep that amused tone in your voice, and somehow along the way switch the conversation to wifey, or the kids. This reminds Mr. Octopus of the comforts of home. Comforts he may not only lose, but have to pay for, should anybody catch him with an overly-enthusiastic arm pinning you to the wall.

Now it's time to wriggle out of his clutches gracefully. Should this be difficult, mention you have to go to the BATHROOM. State matter-of-factly that anchovy hors d'oevres do funny things to your BOWELS. Then clutch your stomach, cross your knees, moan, excuse yourself in a panicky tone, and run to the potty as fast as possible. If you can, make certain to put on enough of a show that several sober adults see you.

Ethelrod will be left thinking "no wonder her husband left her." Then he will depart, which is what you want. Chances are rather good he will not come back. But since you have not slugged him, or kneed him, you can still say "hello" at various board meetings and shopping centers. This is very nice in both the long and short run.

However your trials are far from over. There are still those suave souls who prefer not to operate in the presence of groups to contend with. Instead, they will arrive at your door at 9:00 p.m., using the Just-Happened-To-Be-Passing-By routine.

It's really hard to refuse to let Lothar in, especially if you've been to dinner at Mr. and Mrs. Lothar's house umpteen times. So be tactful and admit your visitor. Assume that Lothar is simply passing by. Your very first comments should be about wifey's well being.

Your conversation might go something like this: "What a co-incidence you happened by! I've been thinking about *Myrna* all day today. How *is* she? You know, I simply adore your *wife*. She couldn't have been more marvelous about baking all those cupcakes for the *church*.

Your comments serve to remind Late-night Lothar of the people who will take note if he doesn't watch where he's stepping right now.

Continue your oratory with, "I've been meaning to call *Myrna* all week, but you stopping by really reminds me I *must* telephone her first thing tomorrow. Your *wife* and I have *so much to talk about.*"

By now, you've stalled long enough to get your wits together. Hopefully, Lothar has too, and will depart for the comforts of a sports rerun in front of his own boob tube. However, if he continues to hold his ground, you will be forced to make a few instant value judgments—which is why you need to get your wits together.

If hearsay, or instinct, even remotely telegraphs that Lothar is a potential troublemaker, do not even let his ingrown toenails past the entry weatherstripping. How do you discourage him even more? The same way you got rid of the salesman who wanted to sell you a nice piece of Florida swamp, or the sweet religious lady who just wanted to chat, or the guy selling you aluminum siding when you were living in an apartment house.

Basically, it's "thanks, but no thanks." Or, as our former First Lady put it, "Just say no." You might mention, depending on the situation, that you don't feel particularly well. Then politely say goodbye, and just as politely deadbolt the door.

A more direct alternative is to moan you have a terrible case of influenza, gag like you're going to vomit, hastily slam the door, and just as hastily lock it. Then retreat to the kitchen, make a consolation prize bean burrito, and wait until you hear Lothar's station wagon pull away.

He won't be overjoyed at your actions, but then chances are Lothar's had doors closed in his face before and will merely add you to his list of women who "don't know what they're missing." Actually, you know full well what you are getting out of, but you have been reasonably tactful, and should you meet Lothar at the local bakery you can always casually mention that you are still taking penicillin for your flu. This keeps the fear in him of catching something, yet preserves civilities.

As a single-again person, you don't have a husband around for real or implied protection. Therefore, you are going to have to learn to be a very good judge of character. Some socially-prominent persons and well-respected neighbors have been known to get their way through rape. You've had enough problems in your life; you don't need any more. So, when in doubt, don't let Late-night Lothar in!

What happens if the Lothar on your doorstep seems like he would qualify for sainthood? For whatever reasons, you are absolutely certain he won't make a pass unless given substantial encouragement. Well, personally, I prefer keeping married men out of the house; period. However, if you choose and it's early in the evening, with all the children clamoring and slobbering about, you can opt to let Lothar in for a cup of coffee. Seat him in the kitchen, not in the living room, leave the television set blaring sitcom reruns and the dog scratching its fleas.

Lothar may stay for coffee and leave, but chances are you'll spot no intention of his ever going home. You can talk about children and cake mixes to the point of nausea, but he will still sit and sit and sit.

Lothar is waiting for the kids to go to bed. He is sitting there hoping against hope that you will encourage him to hold your hand. When you do not do this, he will sit some more.

In this situation, your children can become your best friends. Remind them about the late-night Frankenstein special on TV. Ask them to demonstrate the latest school cheer for your guest. Pass out the double-bubble gum left over from Halloween. But, under no circumstances should you permit your children to leave the kitchen and go to bed. If the sandman threatens to overwhelm them, allow the toddler to fall asleep with her head on the kitchen table. The 5-year-old can fall asleep on the dog. The presence of others provides you with a buffer zone in what can prove to be quite a sitting endurance contest.

Eventually, Lothar will decide you are a terrible mother for letting your little one sit up all night. He may also remember his wife is waiting for him with a tire iron. As soon as he mumbles something like "it's getting late," mobilize your forces immediately. Encourage one bleary-eyed child to carry his raincoat and rubbers to the door. Encourage another bleary-eyed child to hold the door open and let the sleet in. Encourage all the youngsters in a chorus of good-byes loud enough for Santa Claus to hear clear up at the North Pole.

Usually Lothar will leave peacefully. He has offered, in a subtle-macho way, his services. In your own subtle-macha way, you have declined these services. But, since nobody has said anything nasty, you can have dinner with the Lothar family umpteen more times, if you choose, and yet another friendship has been preserved.

A word of caution. Lothar may make one last ditch try right before departing, just in case you didn't understand the true meaning of his impromptu visit. He may start out by coughing, or *harrumphing,* keeping his eyes directed toward the ground. "If you ever need someone to share your burden with," he mutters, "please do let me know. There's a nice little restaurant in X (a town about 75 miles away) where we could talk privately. After all, we've known each other a long time. I want to give you all the emotional support possible during your period of trial and tribulation."

If you're still making every effort to preserve civility, you can pretend to take this offer at face value. "I could discuss it with *Myrna* first thing in the morning," you say sweetly. "If she says okay, I'll definitely keep the idea in mind."

Do not crack a smile as Lothar trembles. Maintain your innocent stance as he hastily comments, "Oh, my wife doesn't care what I do. We have an agreement."

Since this agreement consists of him being allowed to attend Rotary, Elks or Lion's club meetings, where he is likely supposed to be right now, you can confidently repeat, "Well, I'll ask *Myrna* anyhow."

After a few more *harrumphs,* Lothar will drop the subject like a hot potato and make certain the phone is off the hook in the morning. He will also avoid you, perhaps like the plague, for some time to come. However, after a few months, realizing you are not going to blow the whistle on his sainthood, he will begin to feel more at ease. In the interval, he will have said many a prayer that you don't cause any serious problems.

An unfortunate side effect of this is that you will probably be dropped from the Lothar family dinner guest list, if Mr. Lothar can find any excuse for eliminating you. This is not a particularly serious problem, since five-course meals are bad for the waistline anyhow. As a single person, fighting the battle of the bulge is even more important than it was when you were married.

Should you wish to continue your relationship with Myrna, you can always do so when hubby is away at the Rotary Club or on a weekend fishing trip. But keep your mouth shut about her spouse's nocturnal visit. There is an excellent chance he won't show up again, and all you would accomplish by carrying tales is making a nice lady unhappy.

JOB HUNTING IN THE GAME PRESERVE

Looking for a job is really the pits—the second worst in the world. Don't ask me what the worst is, because everybody has their own. Still, nothing's much worse than getting mental heaves in front of strangers, while interviewing for something that appears to pay half the minimum wage. It's totally depressing, and starts from the minute you review your wardrobe—which usually consists of not-so-slimming slacks and cozy "kitchen" dresses. This sorry wardrobe leads directly to the receipt of "sorry not needed" letters based on your maturity factor or a lack of current work experience, perhaps both.

While career counselors tell you volunteerism counts, equal rights enthusiasts talk about applying for managerial positions, and the law says you can't be asked about age, contraceptives, or babysitting arrangements, my experienced response is "Twaddle and Horsefeathers."

If you've gotten husbandly pats on the head for umpteen years in lieu of a paycheck, it's best to be prepared for some of the cow apples that prospective employers will throw down in your footpath to success. A little advance knowledge goes a long way toward preventing hysterics, frustration, and nail biting. Advance knowledge also gives you a chance to formulate appropriate responses to inappropriate questions.

Volunteer Work

Let's say you've been Supermom, able to juggle Girl Scout troops, Junior League, charitable fund-raising committees, house-keeping, and straight-A children without even batting an eyelash.

Proud of your successes, you list under *previous employment* the titles and work done for a plethora of civic minded groups. Then you hand or mail in your resume and wait for a barrage of phone calls. You wait, and wait, and wait. What's the problem?

Employers often feel volunteer work is a far cry from punching an 8:00 a.m. to 5:00 p.m. time clock, five days a week. "Volunteers come and go as they please," said one male personnel officer. "They can, and do, take two hour lunches. They do a lot of social-izing, something not encouraged in an office atmosphere. And if the kids are sick or the repairman is due, with volunteer work there's not a problem with not showing up at all."

You know this is a bunch of malarky. If you have been an effective and consistent group member or coordinator, the experi-ence should qualify you for a delegate's post at the United Nations during wartime conditions. But trying to change preconceived no-tions which are encased in granite takes more spare time than you've got.

There's another little bias too, one which proved quite an eyebrow raiser for a quite-capable, re-entry woman acquaintance when she asked one interviewer why volunteer work seemed to elicit such negative perceptions. "Frankly Mrs. Smythe," the man mumbled, "I feel that anybody who gets involved in so many civic functions just wouldn't have the time or energy to devote to a full-time job."

Statements like this make you want to scream. You may even do so. However, unless you're applying for a yodeler's position, all you'll accomplish is a slight improvement in your lung power, and you'll need that improvement to jog hither and yon in search of an employer with a grain of common sense.

Men are allowed to juggle men's groups, politics and a full-time job. For this they get admiration and applause. Women are often discounted because they have done unpaid labor. So, you need to come up with paid work experience. We'll look at that goal in the next few pages. But first, let's deal with the notion of applying for managerial positions, which pay semi-livable wages.

Managerial Positions

Despite the rosy words coming out of the newspaper women's pages, genuine upper echelon positions are still hard to come by. Hope is always raised by the knowledge that employers, faced with stringent equal opportunity regulations, have to hire a certain number of female persons to fill a percentage of work slots.

Unfortunately, a lot of employers get around the rules by juggling titles. You become an *administrative assistant* rather than a *secretary.* You become a *project coordinator* rather than a *go-fer.* This gets the employer off the hook, but can leave you dangling in a dead-end job at minuscule wages.

Given what is actually, rather than theoretically, available in well-paid job slots, you are in direct competition with women who have managed to work their way up through the ranks. This includes those who have earned MBA's, and have an aggressiveness learned at the business-school of hard knocks.

That's stiff competition for the re-entry woman whose stomach ties up in knots at the mere thought of job hunting. This is especially true if your education ended with high school, or your second year as a college English major with a poetry minor. Sometimes your confidence level, as mine was, reaches such lows that you couldn't peddle steak to a hungry wolfhound.

This doesn't mean you should stop applying for jobs listed as "President—Megabucks Corporation." After all, people do win the lottery. Besides, it's good for you to fill out employment applications and learn to be creative. A friend of mine, who sent out a "zillion resumes," became so skilled at the art that she started her own business doing resumes for other people. Now she is hiring, instead of hoping to be hired. There are always silver linings in what appears to be a bank of dark clouds.

Who's Watching the Kids?

You haven't truly lived until some prospective employer looks you in the eye and asks, "Do you really think you can cope with homemaking duties and a job?" While this is strictly against government regulations, it happens in so many places that it's best to anticipate it. If you don't, you are going to blow your cool in scads of color-coordinated interview suites, none of which color coordinate with the angry red of your face. Anger, although justified, merely serves to confirm the interviewer's impression that mothers should stay home with the children because work makes them too temperamental.

My friend Margie, quite capable of juggling any number of tasks with one hand, while flipping impeccable crepe suzettes with the other, once applied for a job at a major manufacturing firm. In her own words, "The wimpy personnel officer, who came up to my waist, read my qualifications aloud as I sat there. From time to time he nodded, and even occasionally looked impressed. And my credentials are impressive, if I say so myself.

"Just as I thought the position was sewed up, he paused and asked, 'Do you have any children?' I replied that their ages were 7 and 12, they were in school all day, and what did that have to do with anything? To which he responded, 'I want to know what your babysitting arrangements are in case the kids get sick and can't go to school.'"

Margie stood up to her full 5'9", walked around to where the interviewer was sitting, and poked her sturdy index finger into the middle of his white starched shirt. "Would you ask a man that question?" she demanded.

His response? "You certainly have a hostile personality." Margie filed a complaint with the company involved, plus a complaint with the fair employment practices board. However she didn't get the job, which might have been hers if she still wanted it.

You Pay Agencies

As you run your eager fingers down newspaper classified sections, you may see headings such as "Administrative Secretary—

needed now." "Industrial workers—needed now." "Bookkeeper—needed now."

In somewhat fine print, the job is described in glowing detail, including a super salary. You look for the name of the hiring company. It isn't there. Instead, you're urged to call PQT agency and ask for "Betty," "Sandi," or "Eileen." Just before you reach for the telephone, you notice one little word almost overlooked by your enthusiasm. That word is "fee." What does it mean?

Depending on the state you live in, and by approximate definition only, *fee* means you must agree to pay a percentage, or all, of your first month's salary to the agency. The amount will be collected directly from the employer; i.e. you will never see it. So you must figure on a 25 percent, 50 percent, or 100 percent deduction from your initial gross paycheck.

Upon entering the agency, you will be greeted, for perhaps the first time in your job-hunting stint, by a really friendly welcoming person. Your bottomed-out spirits will be cheered by the thought that somebody in this world has the brains to recognize your innate talents. With mounting enthusiasm, you fill out the spate of detailed forms, mentioning all your current skills. Next comes the interview session, where you discuss the type of position you deserve, would like to have, would take at the minimum.

Unfortunately, the position advertised in the newspaper has already been filled. By law, in most states, there has to have been a job opening as described, but the legal minutiae don't exactly specify that the opening can't be closed before the ad hits the paper.

The interviewer's next remark eases your obvious disappointment. She does happen to have quite a few other opportunities for someone with your skill. These don't exactly match the lucrative stipend offered in the newspaper ad for the luring job, but since you got this far you might as well listen. However, many of the unfamiliar buzz words flip right over your naive head. Still, some of the jobs do sound interesting. So you begin asking for specifics.

The interviewer describes the cozy atmosphere, the employer who's a real "jewel," the excellent start you are getting on a promising career track, and the decent salary that will be yours as soon as you "prove yourself."

Figuring you might as well jump in with both feet, you agree to go on on several interviews. This you do, your heart making like a trip hammer. To your amazement, you are offered a position at all three of the places you visit. That's really batting 100.

You do begin to wonder why the job duties mentioned by each prospective employer bear little similarity to what you requested from the agency in terms of hours, days, skills needed, or salary. But now wanted by all, where only a short while ago you were wanted by none, your elation is so boundless that you forget all about such trivia. The future will take care of itself.

The future, however, is a variable. By lucky chance, you may hit upon a solid gold opportunity. With your big toe in the door, you wriggle your size 10C foot in, then perhaps rise rapidly through the company ranks. Soon they are sending you on expense-paid junkets to the Orient, anyplace there's glasnost, plus Paris as a side trip. Just the thought of it makes me want to quit typing and sign up at my nearest fee agency.

There is a glitch in the picture though. Many of my acquaintances, having gone the fee agency route, report super-size headaches. "The place was absolute chaos," Ruth commented. "I was hired to type, but there was no typewriter. It had not been 'sent out for repair,' either. Instead, my position consisted mostly of carrying boxes from one section of the plant to another. I was also assigned to file old charts which must have been untouched since the Spanish-American War."

After working there a few weeks, Ruth discovered that her position had been held by eight different people in the past three months. All of them quit without notice. After a few weeks, she did the same thing.

Ruth went back to the fee agency. She told them her problems, was met with sympathy, and sent out on more interviews. As before, all the prospective employers seemed eager for her services. She accepted another position. This time she didn't wait a month and a half to quit. How did this affect the money she owed the agency?

"If you leave the first week," says an employment agency owner, "you usually don't have to pay anything. After that, up to three weeks, you pay a percentage. If you stay longer than that, you are generally held for the full amount. It depends entirely on the contract you've signed."

It is definitely worth your while to check the fine print when perusing that contract, as agency requirements vary. Some are generous, some are not. Fee agencies have a definite place in the employment market structure. They offer an excellent opportunity for the woman with a lack of recent work experience to get her toes damp in the modern labor force. But you must keep several things in mind.

The first is that your interviewer earns points for every person she interviews, and for every job interview you do. "Her salary may also be based partially on commission, a concept true in no-fee agencies also," says the agency owner. So you are looked at in terms of the dollar sign. If the agency doesn't have a job available meeting your specifications, they don't want you walking out the door. If you do that, there's a good chance you will try a different agency. So they try to interest you in whatever job openings they have currently available.

The second notion, to quote Ruth, is "realize that a *fee* agency knows exactly why you are willing to accept scarce cash for a job. It is because you are desperate, and they can see you coming a mile away." Ruth continues, "That makes two desperate people, for the places that go with *you pay* agencies are often places that have a terrible time finding workers and/or keeping them. This is why they are so eager to see you. You are a live body that can filled the space offered and, hopefully, get some work done."

Ruth admits she has a negative view of fee agencies. However, she also admits that the time and money wasn't exactly wasted. "I got hands-on experience, learned current terminology, and gained skills interacting with other employees," she says. "This all proved quite helpful when I eventually went out looking for a job on my own."

Ruth also learned to be more particular about the type of position she accepted. This was valuable know-how as she advanced in her career, acquiring more hard-earned knowledge as she went. You, too, will benefit from such experience.

Fee agencies may not win prizes, but for the woman approaching the job market scared half to death, they do offer a fairly good chance of getting some type of employment to put on a resume, plus money to pay the landlord and the grocer.

No-Fee Agencies

In a *no-fee temporary placement* agency, the employer pays the agency a finder's fee for securing their labor force. This fee does not come from your paycheck. It is a percentage of what you make, usually about ¼ to ⅓. For example, if you are earning $9 an hour, the company is getting paid $3 an hour for lending you out. This may vary considerably, with most agencies getting a ⅓ cut of the take. All that interests you is what you are making. The rest covers agency costs and profit.

Increasing numbers of small and very large firms are utilizing employment agencies. As a result, employment agencies are springing up everywhere. There are several reasons for this increase.

Personnel managers save time by turning the initial screening process over to employment agencies. Some medium size companies have even done away with personnel people altogether, and only hire through employment agencies.

Many companies use temporary employment agencies as a guard against having to pay unemployment compensation should business go slack. There are no layoffs, you just return to the agency.

Companies hiring through agencies also don't have to pay benefits. Some employment agencies offer these. The terms vary, so ask about them. One large company has almost a year's waiting period before you get benefits. And if you take time off in the middle of the year for anything, you start at day one for eligibility when you return. Another agency has only a 30-day waiting period. Another agency doesn't offer any benefits. Again, ask.

As a side-note, some firms may use employment agencies to screen out applicants they don't want because of age, color, shape, size or handicap. If you think this many be a problem, ask around. As mentioned, there are many agencies. One I know of specializes in the older woman, for example. They feel she's more reliable. Another group is a disability advocate and up on the laws. The longer you are in the market, the more you will learn about these important matters.

Since no-fee agencies only get paid when you get paid, they try harder to place the job hunter in a decent niche. This is particularly true if you are a good worker, doing such things as showing up on time.

A word of caution: be very careful that the no-fee agency is exactly what it says. You are not to pay any monies for being sent out on job interviews. Nor are you to pay upon receiving a job. Nor will you part with any cash if the job you take turns out to be unsatisfactory.

Some alleged no-fee agencies have fee positions. You can be lured in by one and end up with the other. You may be approached with this by, "Well, we do have several other openings. Because they're more desirable, we have a separate contract, etc."

Read all contracts before you sign them. If you don't quite get the drift, or feel somewhat overwhelmed, ask if you can take a copy of the contract home to review more carefully. If the multi-syllabic words are still too much for you, consult with a friend, neighbor, or local advocate. Underline what you don't understand. Then go back to the agency and ask about those underlines. Jot down notes on what you are told, so if there's a misunderstanding later on, you can always pull out your written file.

I am constantly amazed at how many people will sign a multiple page document without doing more than casually scanning the opening and closing lines. This is an open invitation to be misled.

As a newcomer to the game, you will wonder whether asking too many questions makes you seem even stupider than you privately think you are. This is not so. Any agency interviewer worth her salt is going to be glad to answer your queries. If she doesn't have the information, she should be equally glad to pick up the phone and get if for you.

Don't accept a calming, "Let us take care of these minor details." If you do, you're apt to be mired in those teensie details while on the job itself. My friend Eileen, who upon hearing of the salary offered for a bookkeeper at a local nursing home, got so excited she just grabbed the address from the agency and ran before anyone changed their mind about this opportunity.

"So I arrived the very next day at 8:00 a.m.," she recalls. Since the administrator was on temporary leave of absence, i.e. in the hospital for a drying-out cure, and the secretary was also new, nobody was sure of what I was supposed to do. Finally, some lady, who turned out to be the administrator's wife, showed up and shoved an enormous stack of papers in front of me. Their bookkeeper had left abruptly some weeks ago, leaving work piled up from before and after she departed.

"I started sifting through the verbiage. Then it turned out I was supposed to juggle the telephone lines when they got hectic. It also turned out I was supposed to do 'light' typing in my 'spare' time. My spare time was nonexistent, as were my coffee and lunch breaks. I got strict instructions not to chew my sandwich so loudly while answering the phone during my lunch break.

"Despite it all, I managed to get several pages done of what was described as my actual work. The administrator's wife perused these in great detail. Upon completion, she said, 'Well, it seems like you have some idea of what this is all about. So I think we should be able to finish the project up in no time at all. Of course, as you are well aware, we are a bit behind in our billing (this was an understatement). Therefore, you'll be working Saturdays for a while in addition to your regular 7:00 a.m. to 6:00 p.m. day.' (Who? Me? When? Where? That isn't what I was told.)

Eileen stuck it out for two months, since she didn't want to report back to the agency as a *failure*. She also lost ten pounds from aggravation, and got her first case of acne since she was a teenager. Eventually enough was enough, and she returned to the agency with a long list of gripes. At this point she was told, "If you had just asked, we would have told you. As it was, we presumed you didn't care."

And so, like many re-entry women, Eileen had to re-learn a lot about people, herself, and what questions to ask before saying "yes." Questions should cover working conditions, hours, specific job duties, possibility of overtime, paid or unpaid overtime, the name of your direct supervisor, benefits available, etc.

In case you're curious, Eileen eventually did quite well. She stuck it out with one of the agencies she went to, zigzagging through learning procedures. The last time I saw her, she was comfortably ensconced as the sole female in a local trucking firm doing light accounting and dispatch. She was enjoying herself thoroughly, too.

Why Use a Temporary Agency to Get Started?

The basic concept of a temporary agency is to place people for long or short periods of time in places that need vacation relief, busy season assistance, or to fill a recently vacated or new job slot. With the trend toward hiring temporaries rather than permanent personnel increasing, some "temporaries" have remained in a job for five years.

Payment for your services goes to the agency. You are employed by the agency, even though you work for one or many companies. Wages vary with your skills, what the agency can extract from the company, and what the agency thinks you will accept. Some agencies are very good, others are exceedingly slovenly. I have worked at both types. Most are someplace in the middle.

As mentioned, some agencies pay benefits, others don't. Of those that do, some have protracted eligibility periods. The pay differential between one agency and the next does not take into account whether benefits are paid. This is something you must figure out when working with that agency, and calculate it into your salary.

Some people scorn temporary work. There are equally as many re-entry people who say that being able to go from job to job, under agency tutelage, is the best thing that ever happened to them. Let's look at some of the pluses of temporary employment hopscotch:

1) You pick up a bit of this skill and a tad of that skill, in every differing position you handle.

2) You get a thorough inside look at varying jobs and job titles.

3) If you can't stomach your boss, atmosphere, or coworkers at a particular job, you are not stuck there nor do you have the trauma of quitting.

4) You can control your working days and hours to some extent. For example, if you want to vacation the fourth week in every third month, just tell the temporary agency in advance. They may forget, but you don't have to accept any job offers during this period.

5) By travelling around, often in several cities, and keeping your eyes and ears open, you can pick up job leads. Sometimes they're at the company you're working for, since people quit all the time.

37

6) You cannot be fired by the company that hires you from the temporary agency. They can tell the agency they don't want you back again. They can tell the agency, and they do, that they prefer 5'3" blondes over 5'9" brunettes. They can tell the agency that you refused to work overtime and through lunch. But they can't give you that dreaded *pink* slip, the thought of which induces migraines in many a wage earner. Even if the employer complains, case-hardened agency personnel, accustomed to personal idiosyncrasies, merely sigh and place you someplace else. Of course, if the gripes come fast and hard from multiple employers, your talents and working disposition are apt to get a second and even third look from the agency.

7) By being, on occasion, placed in positions you never dreamed existed back in your happy-housewife days, you may just find yourself settling into a comfortable career. For example, one woman I interviewed started at a paint manufacturing company as a temporary secretary. Her only experience with paint was finger painting as a child and trying to paint the bathroom at home sky blue, but she was interested, willing to learn, and curious enough to ask questions. The lady not only stayed on, she moved up. Last I heard, she was plant manager, and it didn't take all that long.

In general, many people find temporary agencies a good way to get re-acquainted with the working world with the least amount of trouble. If you are opting for the secretarial market, and worried about deteriorating typing skills or nonexistent computer skills, some agencies have training programs. Ask about them, as they may not be mentioned by staff.

There are, of course, drawbacks to temporary agencies. You may be drop-kicked into jobs that have no relation whatsoever to your skills. This may be your fault for boasting unduly, the agency's fault for not paying attention to what you told them, or the employer's fault for not giving an accurate description of job needs. In most instances, although you tend to blame the agency, it is the employer's fault for providing a poor job description. An agency can only work with the information it is given.

Once, when I was working as a temp, I was sent out on a temporary typist position for a building firm. Within 10 seconds of my arrival, I discovered they wanted statistical tabulations. My experience there was zilch, but being a stubborn person, and given the state of the art in most offices today, I was able to fool around while looking diligent, and eventually managed to get the drift of tabulation statistics.

While regular staff polished fingernails and gossiped, I worked straight through. I finished that day's assignment and the next day's too. However, there is no happy ending to this tale. Since I finished the next day's work, they didn't call me back the next day. I have since learned super efficiency doesn't always pay, and so sometimes hold back the talent except when I'm working for myself.

Another drawback to temporary agencies can be the pay, although, as they are increasingly relied upon by business, the pay is going up. However, as you acquire good computer and word processing skills, you can advance yourself mightily along the monetary trail. Sometimes you have to change agencies to do it. Try to meet other *temps*. They'll tell you who pays an honorable wage.

Women who enter as temporaries, beginning with very brief assignments, then going on to spend six months or more in one place, tend to progress to good salaried positions. Susan, after 20 years of home life, had been told she was "qualified to hash at the local beanery." Her varicose veins found the thought intolerable. She began looking for a sitting job, and finally signed up with a local temporary agency.

The agency sent her, among other places, to a large computer manufacturing firm as a file clerk. Susan took a look at the opportunities posted on the bulletin board, and thought, "If those [fools] an learn to program, I can too."

This she did, wangling as much on-site instruction as possible, then signing up for a programming curriculum at the local junior college. Susan now has a permanent position with the computer company. The position includes a comfortable chair in an air-conditioned office. "And nobody ever tells me I forgot the ketchup," she says with a grin.

At this point, *temporary to permanent* positions should be discussed. Some agencies offer this option, others do not. Generally, if a company wants to promote you from a temporary to a permanent position, they must pay a fee to your agency for the privilege. As mentioned earlier, many places actually utilize temporary agencies for staff screening. If your primary interest is in permanent work, make certain your agency takes on this type of clientele.

"But do keep in mind," warns one agency owner, "that agencies make more money when they keep putting you out as a temp." So if an agency where you have requested permanent work isn't finding you anything approaching your needs, don't hesitate to switch. Most temps work with at least two agencies at any time, just to keep their opportunities coming.

In general, it doesn't seem to matter whether you sign on with a big agency or a small one. Rather, it is the person managing that particular office that is important. Management of temporary agencies suffers the same problem as management of corporations. Some people hustle more than others, some take better care of their employees than others. Once again, shop around and ask other temporary workers.

Help Wanted Ads

It takes a great deal of courage, and a certain willingness to play *hide and seek,* to chuck the support system offered by the various types of employment agencies and go it alone via the "Help Wanted" section of your local newspapers.

Let's say you want to be a writer. Opportunities may be listed under any of the following headings: writer, freelance writer, journalist, public relations, editor, editorial assistant, publicity director, reporter, technical writer, copywriter, marketing director, newsletter editor, or communications coordinator.

There are also positions requiring skilled writing ability listed under administrative assistant and general secretary. When you start looking through the classifieds, begin with *Aardvark* and conclude with *Zyzzyva.* Yes, read the section from beginning to end.

Aside from interfering with your favorite television program, thoroughness has decided advantages, You're not only perusing the fine print, you're also looking at positions you might never have considered otherwise. Keep an open mind, or you might miss a true diamond in the rough.

For example, you've got teaching credentials and some experience. You're not really keen on teacher stress again, but you look through "teachers wanted," "educators wanted," and "instructors wanted." The openings are too far from home, the salaries don't cover your home heating bill, and the subjects are outside your field of expertise.

If you have an open mind, you will take note of ads that read, "Supervisor needed, chemical manufacturing firm. Must have ability to work with, and instruct, people of varying educational and ethnic backgrounds. Teaching experience a definite plus. On-site training provided."

Many firms like to hire former teachers. "They have nerves of steel," one executive quipped. A corporate job can provide good income and an upward track, so keep an eye out for the options.

When you read "help wanted" ads, put a red check mark by all those you think you might be remotely qualified to hold. After a while, you will find the check marks form a definite pattern. They also increase your confidence. In all likelihood, you have talents that can be expanded to cover jobs that you might previously not have considered. Follow up the doodles with a phone call or revised resume. You never know if you suit the other person's needs for the job unless you try.

What happens if you don't find anything in the local newspaper? By all means shove a few more quarters in *all* the newspaper dispensing kiosks, including the Wall Street Journal. Employers place ads in the oddest places, and newspapers from neighboring cities may have ads for your city because the parent firm has a branch there or because they're reaching out for applicants to meet EEOC regulations.

If the idea of buying several newspapers each day terrifies your budget, cut expenses by limiting yourself to the Wednesday and Sunday editions. These generally have the best classified sections. They also have money-saving coupons which generally defray the newspaper's cost.

Another place to find newspapers is your local library. They get batches each day from your city and from major cities nearby, and there's no cost to the reader. Just make certain to take pen and paper to copy all the information, or enough coins to feed the copy machine.

There are also other sources for job listings besides the newspaper. Mention and re-mention to all your friends that you are looking for work. They may know of somebody that needs somebody. I know of one woman who started in the florist business this way. Another woman landed an entry-level position in an electronics firm and progressed from there. There are times you will feel like a royal pest mentioning your job search, but word of mouth is the best sourcebook there is.

You may also want to check bulletin boards outside the local college employment office. If you are a student, or have ever been a student at that college, even part-time, you are usually eligible for the services provided. Call and ask if you're not sure. You might also be eligible for job counseling, an added bonus.

Government agencies, and various other corporations, often list their openings on flyers that go into large loose-leaf employment books which must be made available at public sites. Such sites include the unemployment office, library, and college employment office.

Civil service jobs usually pay pretty well, and therefore have a waiting list. You will have to take a basic skills test. If you pass that, you will be called in for an interview. Then a few months to two years may pass before you hear from anybody. Apply for anything in civil service you think you qualify for, and take all the exams. Do this often enough and you will get a job.

Persistence Pays

It is absolutely essential to go to as many interviews as you can manage. At first, you don't even have to be extremely interested in the job. In fact, if you're not interested, it helps you stay calmer.

When I was job hunting, I got so horridly depressed that I asked a girlfriend, who had once made a living selling mops and brooms door to door, how she kept from getting discouraged at the inevitable rejections. "Set yourself a goal," Corinne replied, "such as twenty interviews. By the twentieth, you'll get the job you want."

I remember scoffing at the advice, but desperate for any straw to hang on to, I took it anyhow. So when I saw an ad on the college bulletin board for a "shopping center promotion director," I applied. I knew next to nothing about what the job entailed, but figured it was interview number fourteen toward my goal of twenty. At that time, I was trying to become an editor, and nothing else held much interest. But I did need money in my checking account.

Perhaps because I didn't actually want the job, I was calm, cool and collected instead of castanet kneed. Apparently my serene demeanor was in marked contrast to that of the other applicants, because I was hired almost immediately.

The job, which I took while waiting for a better one, turned out to be a tremendous growth opportunity. It really honed my writing skills and media contacts. I didn't expect to be there six months, but I stayed four years.

Ask anyone you know how they got their current position. You'll hear some interesting, way-out stories, get some rather clever ideas, and have a few chuckles besides.

From Lisa: "I had been doing entry-level secretarial work and the pay was ... awful. So while plodding away, I kept looking for a chance to improve myself. By keeping my ears open, I learned there was a tremendous need for people willing to type numbers. I had been to the personnel office of the neighboring defense plant on several occasions, but this time I casually mentioned that I was crazy about typing numbers. The gal at the desk, who had been totally ignoring me, suddenly came alive. I had a phone call one hour after arriving home, and started work at triple my prior salary."

From Julie: "I had applied and applied for a job, any type of office work. But nobody would even consider me. I was either over qualified, under qualified, or lacked recent work experience, etc. Finally I woke up and smelled the mustard. The next time I filled out a job application form, instead of using my married name, Julie Ann Smith, I used my maiden name, Julie Gonzalez Smith. I received job offerings from both places where I did this."

From Terri: "I had been rather abruptly fired from a good copy-editing position merely because the boss's new daughter-in-law wanted my job. However, I did get unemployment benefits out of it. This included placement services and basic job counseling as well as a regular check. ... I went out on a bunch of miserable interviews. Instead of getting discouraged, I badgered the counselor for more job leads. After a couple of months I began to look like a permanent fixture in the unemployment office. I guess my counselor thought so too, because one day she mentioned, 'We have an opening in the unemployment office. Are you interested?' I was, and took the test. I've been here ten years now and really like it. I started as an entry-level clerk and now I'm a supervisor."

These are typical stories. You, regardless of age, have something to offer that somebody wants. Don't figure you can't do any type of job until you've tried it. All you can do is get fired, and that happens to the best of us from time to time, even though we don't always admit it. There's an automobile tycoon whose charisma rests on getting canned and rising to a six-figure salary within a short time. Maybe you have read one of his success books?

Those Awful Interview Questions

While being interviewed, chances are you will have to cope with a series of seemingly-stupid questions. Some of these, particularly in major firms, are written out in check-list form for the interviewer. This can reduce you to complete mush.

Regardless of internal turmoil, always resist the temptation to punch the interviewer in the nose. This not only damages your delicate hands, but can result in bloodstains on your new business suit. Besides, the interviewer may actually be trying to do a good job. It's not her fault that company policy reads a certain way. Instead, make it your business to learn proper replies, otherwise known as the *fudge factor.*

Take the inevitable stupid question, "What are your goals?" You don't want to say pay the rent, buy the kids sneakers, or get a new perm at the local beauty school. At times, I have been tempted to say, "My goal is to be the next president of IBM," but of course that just doesn't do.

Instead, use whatever seems to fit into their obvious check list. "Work to better the organization," is nice. "Manage my own department," is good. You may have to prevaricate a bit.

The person interviewing you may be thinking of his personal problems and not even truly listening to you. So, if you give what appears to be a sincere answer, you can usually escape this opening hook.

The next nuisance question concerns money, as "What type of salary are you expecting?" It would be nice to say, "Six million dollars a year plus perks, ho, ho," but this doesn't go over too well.

Nor does vastly overestimating salary. I lost a potential job once because I aimed at a grand more than the interviewer's typed list limit. In reality I would have taken anything just to get a leg in the door. But it's hard to figure out what to say if the salary hasn't been mentioned in the company's advertisement.

If you can, before you go in for the interview, try to get some ballpark figures from news paper ads for comparative job titles. Say a secretarial job pays between $18,000 and $26,000 a year within your city and several neighboring ones. Take a good look at your skills and background. What's your minimum need? What are you willing to settle for and still be happy? When you are asked the salary question, you can say, "a range between $20,000 and $23,000 per year, depending on opportunities for advancement." Or you can fudge a bit and say, "I'm willing to negotiate on salary if working conditions are satisfactory."

If the offer is so low it wouldn't support a family of sparrows, it's best to avoid saying, "You flintstone cheapskates. You have a lot of nerve." Although, I know somebody who did this once. She really felt better afterward.

Actually, I did something like that once, too. I had gone out for a job advertising a "competitive salary." I knew what the going rate was for this particular position, so I made the rather lengthy drive to the site. When I got there, spent half an hour in interviews, and then heard the salary, my reflex reaction was, "If you had told me that in the first place, I never would have bothered to come here." The fellow looked irate, but it was true; it was a waste of my time, and his too.

You should inquire about perks with any job. Health, dental, and life insurance, pension plans, sick leave, investment options, and child care on-site are just a few of the hidden factors in a salary. Some companies even pay college tuition, if the courses pertain to your job. All this is worth quite a bit of money, so ask, ask, ask. Benefits can mean a difference of several thousand dollars per year. Add up the total package before you turn a job down.

All the while you're talking, the interviewer will be sneaking glances at your application form. Like it or not, you will get at least one general question about prior work experience. If you have put down something legitimate, the answer is relatively simple. You mention positive skills utilized on the job or jobs. Throw in words like "efficiency," "reliability," and "ability to work well with diverse groups of people." The latter is important because most companies have their share of lunatic fringe, plus a modern array of ethnic groups. Your noted ability to keep cool, especially if you're from an ethnic group yourself, is a decided plus factor.

If you've used the *fudge factor* on your application form and put down "two years of typing" for your ex-husband's office, or perhaps you've written that you managed Daddy's cigar factory for a dozen years than it gets a bit more complicated.

If you've had anything to do with the job you've listed, even if it's just evening chats with once-husband or Daddy, you have probably learned some key phrases. Even these are more than the interviewer knows about many jobs. So keep your answers simple and general, emphasizing skills you already have. It also helps if, for character reference, you have included at least one clergy member.

Suppose you have been fired from your prior job? Never bad mouth previous employers. The interviewer will start believing you might say the same nasties about his precious firm. Instead, say, "The job was quite interesting (which covers a multitude of sins), but my position was terminated due to change in management." Everybody knows new management brings along instant turnover. The interviewer will usually drop the whole distressing matter, perhaps having faced it himself/herself at one time or another.

Perhaps the problem isn't prior work experience, but just that you've been out of work for a somewhat lengthy period. You're afraid the job gap makes it look like nobody sane would hire you. Many people use "self-employed" to bridge the time periods. Legitimately self-employed persons get very annoyed at this tactic, but it's done all the time. If you don't like to fib, take a try at peddling lipsticks, detergents or algae vitamin pills. Then you're not fibbing, have a basic idea of what you're talking about, and may even find you like sales, a very lucrative career field.

It's been repeatedly documented that there is little backchecking done on past employment. If the interviewer likes you, or needs somebody "right now," there is a minimal background check. Besides, people have a tendency to sue former employers for written criticisms that costs them a job and which cannot be proven by a multitude of paperwork and witnesses. The interviewer knows this. Yes, he or she can make a casual phone call, which is the way it's done these days, but even that is a lot of trouble, and can result in a lot of problems. So that might not be done either, particularly for an entry-level position.

It's worth taking a chance, particularly if there's no other way to land a current opportunity, and past honesty hasn't been rewarded. All you can lose is face, and you might get the job. In the long run, the company can have a very good, loyal employee. You.

There are also questions that *don't* appear on the official printed company form. One which crops up with dismal regularity is an offhand, or obnoxiously direct, remark about child care or "how many kiddies?"

I lost a promising position once because I brought several copies of my well-written articles on family life to a journalism-related interview. In one of the articles, I humorously described how my child-rearing practices differed for each of my four children.

The interviewer, a young woman, scanned the industrial articles. But when she came to the child-rearing article, her eyebrows arched. "How will you ever cope with this job and all your other responsibilities?" she asked in amazement. (How would I ever cope with starvation, I wanted to say. My kids were, as always, well cared for.) The interview was, for all intents and purposes, over, even though it dragged on for another half hour.

Eventually I learned to relieve the interviewer of having to ask such an illegal question in the first place. For example, I managed to interject, someplace along the way, the following statement, "Now that my eldest daughter is getting ready to enter college, I have ample free time to increase my job opportunities." On occasion, I followed that up by mentioning my "other daughter, who is getting ready to graduate from high school." Then I rapidly changed the subject.

The interviewer presumed there were only two daughters, both on the verge of adulthood. She or he also presumed I was a little older than I looked, married very young, or had stepchildren. Either way, child care obviously was not a problem and the subject didn't arise again. Usually the interviewer looked rather relieved.

Notice, too, that I haven't told any real lies. My eldest daughter, at the time, was getting ready to enter college in about three years. Her sister, age 12, couldn't wait to graduate from high school. If I neglected to mention the 10-year-old, or the 4-year-old, it can be laid at the door of absentmindedness. And since nobody bothered to delve deeper, particularly when I quickly changed the subject, the topic zigzagged onto something else.

A friend, with young twin boys, chastised me for all this verbal footwork. "It's too complicated for me," Sarah said. She tried another tack, after being eliminated from a series of job opportunities following kiddycare questions. When an older woman interviewer asked her whether there was somebody reliable to watch the children. Sarah shot back, "Were your children every neglected when you went back to work?" It was a show stopper, and she got a smile and the job.

Other women have offered alternate suggestions. "My grandmother provides day care," is one. Or you can state that an aunt lives next door, or that you share quarters with a sister that just dotes on children. I know several lucky people who have just these situations, so it's possible.

Remember, nobody asks a man, even one with child custody, about his babysitter problems, or what he will do if the youngsters get chickenpox. Until this query crops up as often for males as it does for females, you can give any freeflowing answer you choose. Should you happen to trip over it later on, you can always says "the situation has changed since I got hired."

Equipment Fears

Modern technology means rapid change in machinery. There's a natural fear in tackling complex equipment, if you've been out of the job market a long time.

Recently, an acquaintance confided to me that she wanted to quit her job as a department store salesperson and go back to being a dental assistant. But it had bcen so many years since her school days, she didn't think she could handle the whatzamajiggers that dental assistants currently handle. This woman is competent, intelligent and quick to learn. To her, and to you, I say "onward and upward."

Take a tour of that office, factory, or wherever you want to work. If the person you see operating the gadgets in question doesn't look any swifter than you feel, then you too can manipulate the same little buttons and levers, and with a bit of practice get the same or better results.

If you really feel out-of-touch, inquire about brush up courses. Evening schools, ROP (Regional Occupational Programs) classes, business schools, college extension programs, private programs, all give brush up courses at varying costs. You may be surprised at how inexpensively you can learn, and how easily you can get a grant or loan.

If you are just somewhat out of touch, you just might be able to brush up on the job. My standard ploy was to say that the equipment at my last position was a little different, and to suggest that there are many different models. (This is America, the home of the import, so there *are* many different models of everything.) Then I ask if they would mind giving me a brief review, so I can do it exactly the way they like.

Whoever is in charge is usually quite happy to give you a review. This gives them a chance to demonstrate superiority and also prevents you from pushing the wrong button and blowing the expensive gizmo right through the acoustical ceiling.

Should you not understand instructions the first time, ask again. If you think asking twice suggests a failing on your part, wait until the person in charge is out of sight and ask somebody else. Now you're in a better position, since you're equipped with basic terminology and rudimentary ability. Your inquiries sound more intelligent already.

Take note of the possibility that one reason you may not have understood the instructions was the person teaching you didn't know what he or she was talking about. They may have glossed over things they didn't fully understand and given you a scornful look if you asked them to elaborate. Don't feel bad about your learning ability, and watch out for this person who may realize you know *the truth* about their talents.

As you master the assigned contraption, see what else you can learn to operate. Now you're under no particular pressure, so you can be more relaxed about asking coworkers for how-to tips. You can also discreetly inquire whether the company has any advanced training courses in anything. A good employer is pleased to have an employee who believes in self-improvement. If your employer isn't supportive, scoot back to school anyhow. Get the additional skills you need to increase your own sense of self-confidence.

There is a certain timidity that develops in women, educated or not, who have stayed home for umpteen years. There can be extensive community service work, superb lifestyle efficiency, and demonstrated creative skills, but when faced with the outside job market there's a distinct lack of self-confidence. Many disastrous marriages continue long past a logical dissolving point primarily so the male can be relied on for a paycheck (among other psychological reliance factors).

Yet sometimes there comes a day, willing or unwilling, when you have to provide your own security blanket. Maybe that's why you're reading this book now. You're dragging out your rusty survival weapons from forgotten hiding places and getting ready to go out job hunting in the game preserve. Along the way you may encounter a few pythons, a couple of peccaries, and an occasional platypus. But eventually you will bag your job, and it may provide more than a security blanket.

You will bring home a cache of "I can do it," and "Maybe I'm not so slow," and "Gee, I'm getting better all the time." It's a very exhilarating feeling, although it takes some time to settle in. When you know that you can earn a living, and don't have to rely upon spousal whims for support, a self-confidence takes hold that never leaves you. And it is very nice indeed.

NICKEL AND DIMING IT

There is an inflexible rule which says that two weeks after hubby disappears, the refrigerator will die of old age, the dishwasher will bake on dirt rather than wash it off, and your trusty Model Q Ford will develop at least two bald tires.

After you have stomped around the house for a while, waving your hands, stamping your feet, and dredging up curses learned from your children, you will take out your checkbook and start adding it up again hoping you made an error in your favor. This is seldom the case, and you frequently discover that the electric bill you recently paid was never entered at all.

This gives you perhaps 70 cents to get to the end of the month, and not only are you out of eggs, you're also out of sanitary napkins. As a single mother, you will soon earn a Ph.D. in thrift. The title of your doctoral dissertation will be "Methods of Changing a Nickel into a Quarter Without Using Black Magic." The dissertation's contents will demonstrate ways to calculate your shopping hours as if you were getting a paycheck for the monies saved. Research will begin at the supermarket, where there are many ways to cut a food budget in half and still have steak on the menu.

Grocery Genius

Have you ever eaten a tasty label? Then stop paying as much as 30 cents a can, and a dollar a box, for fancy wrapping paper and living color photography. Most chain supermarkets offer no frills packaging. These are their own brand of merchandise, and they're usually lower in price than major brands on that very same shelf.

You object? Those who pay attention to television commercials, instead of getting up and dusting, will shudder at the thought of getting *seconds*, that don't come wrapped in glossy promises. After all, XYZ brand of tomatoes, corn, etc., will surely make you youthful, wrinkle-free, and able to leap tall buildings at a single bound. Everybody knows that.

Well, not quite everybody. Often, XYZ company may also manufacture the house, or generic, brand. There's just no million dollar advertising campaign attached to the label, with accompanying costs passed on to the consumer. The can or carton may be slightly less exotic, but the taste is about the same.

If you want to check this out, have your children do a comparison test. Ask them if they can tell XYZ brand from ABC brand. Chances are, whether it's cookies or spinach, they'll find little difference between the generic and the brand name. My little ones even like some generic foods better, particularly the peanut butter, which isn't quite so loaded with sugar.

You're still worried. No frills may be good enough for the youngsters, but what about your gourmet friends due over for dinner Friday night? My friend Christie laughs at this one. A physician's wife, she regularly entertains the community big-wigs. Food and wine flow in abundance. Yet Christie considers herself a very frugal housewife.

"Your liquor bill must be tremendous," I commented one spirited evening. The lady laughed. "It's not a penny more than the minimum," she confided. "You'll notice how everything is in decanters rather than the original bottles. That's because I buy liter jugs of 'El Cheapo' at the market, hide the original containers, and serve it up looking crystal pretty. I've never had a contrary comment, even from wine aficionados."

Christie does gild the lily a bit. She leaves, in full view on her kitchen counter, a few empty bottles of rare and ancient vintage. Guests automatically assume they belong to what they are imbibing. And you can pull this same camouflage trick, or think of your own variations, when you have a party.

For those disliking deception of any kind, or truly addicted to name-brand edibles, there is another alternative. Find your closest dented can haven, a good place to socialize with your equally frugal friends. Dented can warehouses, or you-pack-and-save stores, aren't fancy. They don't have piped in music, color coordinated shopping carts, or floors gleaming with fresh wax. They are also not always located in the fancier neighborhoods. Name brand items are generally stocked, but they may have a torn label, dent in the side, or minor problems. Prices can range up to one-third to one-half off. Meat and frozen products may also be sold here, but I tend to be wary of these, as I'm not certain what the problem is. Lengthy defrosting en route may be one reason the re-frozen product is on sale, and I'd prefer not to take the chance of spoilage.

There are also new discount-by-buying-in-bulk centers, like Costco and Price Club. Some items here are less expensive, some are not. I tend to buy a lot of my junk food here, because it is usually quite a bit cheaper than in other stores: i.e., packaged lasagne, pizza, cupcakes, that type of thing. So guard against spending your savings on silliness.

You can sometimes find food discount centers in the telephone book yellow pages, but I've had limited success with this because names and locations are so variable. My best snooping results come from casually asking around at various social or work coffee klatches. For example, I found one discount site through a neighbor, another via a babysitter. If "asking around" bothers you, mention it's just for a friend. Since a healthy bank account is a friend indeed you are not exactly fibbing, just stretching your verbal talents a bit.

While stretching, don't forget that gasoline monies go farther when you share the driving with a budgeting buddy. If you have a buddy with a pickup truck or station wagon, that's even better. If you don't, make certain the compact car will hold two people's purchases, including impulse items.

Always try to purchase economy size items, if you can do so without risk of spoilage. There are certain food items that seem to disappear almost overnight, as if a horde of hungry ogres have been raiding your pantry. For example, in my household, "Mommy, we don't have anymore …" generally finishes with the words peanut butter, ketchup, or cooking oil. Ingredients that go into Italian and Mexican dishes are also usually in short supply, since they form an integral part of my thrifty weekly meal plan.

If you hesitate to buy in bulk because the kids can't handle large size containers, divide them into smaller ones leftover from something else. Be sure to re-label. A nickel saved here, a nickel saved there, and you're following the same path as many of today's self-made millionaires.

It's more difficult, due to refrigerator space limitations, to purchase perishable items as cheeses or luncheon meats, in the giant size version. Yet savings are still to be had with fresh dairy or deli products.

Larger supermarkets will often offer substantial price cuts toward the end of a product's store selling date, which is stamped (or supposed to be stamped), on the package. Although government regulations restrict product shelf time, the food is still quite edible. Cheese may be slightly drier, but that makes grating easier. Bologna or salami may be good only for three days in your fridge, instead of the usual week, but it never lasts longer than that in my house anyhow.

If you remain squeamish about dated dairy items, but still want savings, you might want to consider making your dairy purchases at an alternate site. There are often local cheese manufacturers where cheese can cost $1.50 less a pound than in the stores, and it's fresher too.

It may not have any fancy wrappers, but I don't eat the wrappers, anyway. I buy twenty pounds at a time, cut it into convenient chunks, and freeze it. If my savings is $1.50 per pound, that's a $30 saving for about fifteen minutes shopping time and whatever driving time it takes. Another payoff here is that this type of cheese tends to freeze and remain fresh, rather than turn into crumbly bits like the supermarket cheeses.

While you're scouting for market bargains, look for the sign that says *Day Old,* either at a special bread rack or in neighborhood bread outlets. Bread prices are cut in half, or more. There are also rolls, cakes, cookies, pies, donuts, pretzels, and assorted chocolate-covered cavity causers. The taste differential between last night at 9:00 p.m. full price, and day old at 8:00 a.m. when the bread appears on the discount rack, is negligible. And some of the items are quite new, the result of overenthusiastic ordering and supermarket shelf overflow.

I have actually seen delivery people come in, place a $1.87 loaf of bread on the regular shelf, run out of space, and place the remainder on the discount shelf. Today I picked up fresh name-brand overstocked hot dog buns for 15 cents a package. That type of bargain makes me actually like grocery shopping!

Let's take a moment and see how this methodology translates into cash. If you purchase six loaves of bread at a 75 cent discount each, that gives you $4.50 take home pay for 30 seconds of non-labor. Spend another 30 seconds, add six packages of sweet rolls at the same discount, and you have now earned $9 a minute. Multiply that by 60 minutes, and it turns into $540 an hour. If you can earn that type of salary anyplace else, please let the world know.

If you're thrifty, your cash flow might allow for steak once in a while, but—as with everything else—why overspend? Early morning shopping is smart shopping at the meat counter of many supermarkets. *Reduced for Quick Sale* can mean a dollar or more off per package. Some markets have a special section at the end of the meat case for this. The best time for hunting is morning. The best days are Sundays or the day after a three-day holiday.

While in supermarkets, don't spend your savings on tempting junk located in the non-food aisles. Today's supermarkets contain appliances, towels, sheets, sneakers, socks, lipsticks, etc. There's a huge markup on these items, so the displays are often quite alluring. Close your eyes, come back tomorrow, play little games with yourself, but don't clutter your shopping cart with impulse purchases.

Paper Products, etc.

Toilet paper disappears in my house as if I am supplying an army platoon. It's quite embarrassing to knock on a neighbor's door and ask if they have a spare roll, and it adds to cost if you have to bribe one of the children to handle the task for you.

A plan-ahead program is necessary for household miscellaneous necessities. In large part, this consists of looking for *loss leader* type specials in local newspaper advertisements.

By rough definition, *loss leaders* are items that stores accept a monetary loss on in order to lure you through their portals to purchase other goods at normal price. Your job is to turn those *loss leaders* into your *profit leaders* by using the *multiple purchase system.*

If toilet paper is normally $1.30 per four-roll package, and is being sold today at 90 cents a package, buy ten packages, or even twenty. It's not heavy, will always be used, and has an exceptionally long storage life.

The same plan-ahead approach goes for dishwasher detergent, soaps, shampoos, toothpaste, envelopes and other non-perishables. Supermarkets have loss leaders, but drug stores often offer even better buys. In the 15 minutes it takes to load your cart, you can save $20, maybe more. Tuck the newly found money away in grandma's sugar bowl, and you can save enough for a family vacation at year's end.

Another source of household necessities is that American institution, the flea market. If you tend to shy away from these city and county "come from everywhere" get-togethers as an outlet for used clothes and stolen bicycles, think again. In an afternoon of small change entrance fees, or free admittances, you can find floor wax, flea powder, sunglasses, detergents, shoe laces, baby powder, cosmetics, and quite a few larger items, plus fresh fruits and vegetables.

You name it, the flea market will probably have it. You'll also save on decreased sales tax on the discount price, an often invisible but potent saving. Even the skeptic should bring along a small shopping cart or carrying basket, and always wear a pair of comfortable walking shoes.

Collecting Coupons

Frankly, I consider coupons a pain in the butt, but I do use them. However, I only use them if the savings is 25 cents or more. And I only use them on items I would normally buy anyhow if the price was right. It's easy, with coupons, to get sidetracked into purchasing a specialty tomato sauce at double price. Be extra cautious here.

I use mail-in refunds more often, but again only if there's a genuine savings. The offer has to be at least 75 cents, and preferably a dollar. Remember to figure in the cost of postage and the envelope as part of the product price, or discount it from the refund, when contemplating whether a mail-in offer is worth your time and energy.

While on the subject of coupons, make it a point to check the grocery bulletin board where considerate store managers place cost-saving or refund ideas. You may even have a featured product already at home, with all its requisite labels—a very cheering checkout thought.

It is possible, as numerous books and magazine articles mention, to save large amounts of money with selective coupon use. There are also coupon clubs, where the ladies get together ever so often and trade off coupons, proof of purchase marks, information, etc. All this takes work and time, but, if you enjoy it, it's a fun, money-saving, friendly hobby.

Household Furnishings

Do you need blankets for the bed? Mats for the bathroom? Review department store prices so you're a savvy shopper, then bee-bop down to your local Salvation Army, St. Vincent de Paul or Goodwill store and pick up these basics for a dollar apiece.

While you're there, check out the lamps, mattresses (all sterilized), couches, dining tables, bedroom sets, and other items you need to fill the empty spaces left by hubby's hasty retreat ... with some of the furniture.

Charity thrift stores are also good hunting grounds for items such as scout uniforms, ski equipment, baby clothes, men's shirts, coats, gloves, flowerpots, cookware, picture frames, aprons, and Halloween items. Frankly, I enjoy browsing in these places so much that I even go when I've no specific purchase in mind. Since some thrift stores, even within the same charity, charge more than others, you've got to visit a few to find your favorite. Take care to avoid the thrift store that isn't actually thrifty. Some charge more than your local department store's sale prices, and without department store return privileges and guarantees! As with any business transaction, you have to know the marketplace in order to get the best value for your money and time.

Speaking of time, if you have a few free hours on a weekend morning, check out the local garage sales for super specials. Your best bet here is when people are moving, or there's been a death in the family and heirs can't handle all the junk Aunty Agnes has accumulated for 90 years.

You'll find fascinating selections of patio furniture, baby gear, kitchen appliances, curtains, tablecloths, bedspreads, tools, and even antiques. One time I picked up two dust-covered, gilt-framed French lithographs, for $5 apiece. A dinner guest, that very evening, offered me $25 apiece for them. I didn't sell, as they looked so pretty, but the offer was very good for my spot-a-bargain ego.

Also, if your children are like mine, they break every other cup while washing it. Garage sales are ideal places to purchase distinctive table settings. Coffee mugs are 25 cents, glassware a dime. You don't have to yell at the kids for kiddy fingers if you can purchase a replacement for less than a pack of chewing gum.

A further helpful hint--if you have a choice of garage sale locations, start with the fancier neighborhood first. There is a tendency to put out for sale everything that's been hanging around the homesite for years. Spend your initial time investment with the folk buying the best to begin with. Prices in the pizzazz section of town aren't usually any higher than in the cracked concrete section. Don't let those gold-plated sportscars in the driveway scare you away.

Eventually you will reach the point where you can drive past a garage sale location, look at the items, and instantly decide whether you want to expend any energy shopping. Should you choose to do so, remember that bargaining is often expected. If you love to bargain, your best luck is after the lunch hour. In the morning, the seller often thinks her old ratty kitchen curtains are worth $25. If you do try to negotiate in the morning, and she tells you how much they cost when new, and you want to hang tough, tell her to compare prices with the Salvation Army or St. Vincent de Paul. You can buy full length decorator curtains there for $5.

If the seller proves stubborn, you can try returning later in the day. Now the alternative is hauling the unsold material inside again, so prices tend to get much lower very quickly. Of course, you take the risk that the merchandise may be sold, but that's the fun of garage sales.

A caution: Stay away from items that tick, such as watches. And be careful about mechanical devices like radios, television sets and stereos. They're often being sold because they blip instead of bloop, and there's a strict no-return, buyer beware policy at garage sales. Even if you test the device on site, that's no guarantee that it works.

I once got stuck with a beautiful watch that didn't run. However, it ran at the garage sale when I carefully listened to it go tick-tick. At home, I discovered that it ticked for 10 minutes, stopped for 10 minutes, etc.

Substituting This for That

There are many household items regarded as necessities which really are not. Paper towels are one of these. For this purpose, use old dishtowels, or sections of old bathroom towels, which can be used repeatedly.

This particular substitution caused some upset with an acquaintance of mine every time our friendship group met at my house for tea and cookies. She'd look at my ancient table, then ask for a paper towel. I would hand her a boiled rag. This went on once a month until she started bringing her own cleaning supplies. Then, when she complained about her budget, I inwardly chuckled.

Another place to cut a few dimes from the expenses is eliminating anything that looks like plastic wrap. Instead, save those vegetable bags you get from the market and the rubber bands from your newspaper.

You'll find this combination unbeatable for holding anything from leftovers to casseroles. I love these bags so much, I even use them to roll my pie crusts. (Put the dough inside the bag, which has been slit up the sides. Roll and peel. No fuss, no muss. Someday somebody will get smart and patent them for just this purpose.)

What else? Some of my most attractive vases come from pretty wine bottles. When I smoked, I used cat food and tuna fish cans covered with leftover contact paper in place of ash trays. Margarine and cream topping tubs are wonderful for any type of food or small item storage. For lamp shades, my cousin purchases inexpensive wicker baskets at garage sales, turns them upside-down, makes a small hole in the bottom, and places them over hanging light bulbs or topless lamps. Keep the wicker away from the hot bulb, as you would any other material.

If you're strapped for curtains, you can hand-sew a hem on those one-of-a-kind flat sheets that most big stores have on super sale. Often, they have designer names. All you have to do is slip them on a rod. Curtain rods are cheap enough (especially at the thrift shops), but you can also make a substitute from thick string.

A little creativity goes a long way toward saving money. For example, if your kitchen chairs are charity shop rejects, desperately needing a fix up job, buy a small can of discounted paint at your nearest home or Sears center. Instead of replacing your chairs, paint them. Cover the seats with thick, washable remnants. They don't have to match. Just get them in color coordinated tones, perhaps to match your bedsheet designer curtains.

I made car seats on the same principle. After pricing them at the store, I bought royal purple fuzzy robe remnants at the sewing shop. Using a darning needle and matching yarn, I sewed new over old. It took several hours sweat labor, but its plush and warm. No talent is needed.

Alternative Sources

Books and magazines can be yours galore, at no cost. Get your reading material from the library. Scout your St. Vincent de Paul, or similar charity, some carry magazines. Ask your friends for their old magazines. I regularly trade my copies of the *National Enquirer* for my girlfriend's *McCall's* and the like. Everybody wants to get rid of old magazines, so you are doing them a favor by taking them.

If you are particularly avid about a subscription to a publication, or a book for your reference shelf, this is a good item to put on your birthday, Christmas, or Mother's Day want list. It beats, by a long shot, those little bottles of fancy cologne that make you wheeze, endless see-through nighties that let your freeze, or charming tooth-pick holders which you can't give away for fear of hurting the donor's feelings.

Let everybody who gives you gifts know about your book list. This will save you from getting four lasagne pans, as I did one time.

I like to re-pot my houseplants, for relaxation. Houseplants cover a multitude of furniture sins, like coffee and water stains, cracks, evidence of 100 years use, etc. They also make your apartment or room look rich. I have them all over the place and few cost me anything.

Sharing a cutting is a good luck omen, so I'm told. It's like casting bread upon the waters. So whenever I see a plant that needs a bit of room, I mention that I would be glad to take a cutting or piece for my place. Most people are pleased to share.

My plants go in containers purchased for 50 cents from thrift stores and 25 cents from garage sales. When I get cuttings, I divide them up, put them in pretty containers, and give the extras away as holiday gifts.

Speaking of holidays, don't forget to purchase your gift wrap the day *after* Christmas. Everything is half-off, and if you get there early you get a choice of the more general interest colors, such as blue, gold, silver, and green. These can be used for any occasion. Buy bows, tape, stickers while you're there.

These are just a few ideas. You'll soon develop your own, probably much more creative and penny pinching. As a reward for your genius, you'll soon have the money for a cheer-up-the-blue-mood shopping spree.

Clothing the Kiddies

When your children are little, mention casually to everybody in the neighborhood, plus second cousins, that hand-me-downs get you excited and you enthusiastically welcome each and every one of them, no matter how odd.

If you don't say something like this, folks cleaning closets tend to think you might be offended by kids clothing that's been washed multiple times. Thinking that, they donate all this good stuff to charity, and you have to go out and buy the exact same items at retail price, or from the charity.

Always remember to say "thank-you" after receiving second-hand goods; even if the item wouldn't serve as window rags, say "thank-you." As a rule of thumb, you will usually find at least one quite usable item per hand-me-down bundle. That may amount to $10 you can use someplace else. And if you want more items on a regular basis, try to persuade Junior to wear one of the donated shirts in front of the giver. That person will now glow with the pride of her good deed and think of you when even better items don't fit her children anymore.

It becomes increasingly more difficult to get children over age eleven to use worn clothing. At this point they become acutely aware of what *everybody else* is wearing. This is especially true if their friends have money from rich or over-indulging parents or grandparents.

What I began doing here was giving my daughters cash gifts for holidays and birthdays. This money was to be used for clothing. While twelve seemed young to me for self-choice, they were old enough to learn to handle money and to be responsible for what they did with it. The first few times, with genuine greenbacks in their hot little palms, my budding financiers tended to blow the whole wad on glitter or something almost useless but quite trendy. But mother stood firm as they got to stare at the trendy item while their faded slacks developed worn spots in unfashionable places.

Once their consciousness develops, youngsters tend to become quite aware of prices. They also develop an eye, just like you, for special sales and bargains. We've started going to discount clothing outlets of major department stores. Driving time varies between a half-hour and an hour from home, so we visit about every three months.

Major store outlets carry their name brands, so it's easy for a youngster to pick up fashionable items similar to what the other children are wearing. The selection is huge, the waiting lines at the dressing rooms are long, and some patience sifting through unsorted material is always needed. However discounts are from 50 to 75 percent off the original price. You'll find skirts for $6, and blouses for $4. And it's all new, so the teenager doesn't feel quite so hand-me-down. Image is important, and once they get the thrill of stretching their gift money to the maximum, they are more pleased than you are.

Discount stores don't always have good buys on shoes, nor the selection of other stores. I still give my offspring money at regular yearly intervals for shoes and sneakers. The first time, the youngster might come home with green 4-inch spike heels. But that only happens once, since she'll end up wearing her comfortable old shoes until the next footwear allotment.

The ability to make independent financial decisions gives children a sense of self-confidence, an awareness of the marketplace, and the know-how to make constructive choices. It is never too early to begin. The above methodology, tested on my older children during junior high school, was applied to my youngest daughter by age six. She's now extremely good in math and, when given $25 shopping money, she easily calculates when the total will hit $24.99.

Of course, I do accompany her on shopping trips, but I've learned to keep my personal choices to myself. Sometimes it's not easy. But since the child has to wear the clothing, not Mommy, it's her prerogative to choose stripes instead of polka-dots. And she gets such pleasure out of that choice!

Mother Looks Pretty

Since you're now out in the job hunting or working world, those yucky slacks and housedresses need replacement. Pizzazz should now enter your life. While some books on living thriftily harp on a few outfits of basic black with alternating scarves, I find I prefer color. It makes me feel happier.

Managing this on a strict budget requires a bit of extra footwork. When you have nothing else exciting to do, cruise through your favorite department stores, noting which ones have respectable, honest markdowns on a regular basis. Then meander through these stores on a once every-other-week basis. Patience is often rewarded. Merchandise must be kept moving, and cost cutting to get last season's merchandise off the rack when new season merchandise comes in results in definite benefits to the sharp buyer.

For example, I spied a stunning burgundy dinner dress for $70. Too much. I didn't even try it on for fear of spending the grocery money. Two weeks later, the dress was 20 percent off. But $56 was still too much for me. Another two weeks passed. The dress was now *special sale* priced at $39. Should I or shouldn't I? I didn't—because I couldn't justify another cocktail dress in my closet. But when the department store had a one-day half-price sale, I was there with bells on. The dress was now $19, and all mine.

A tip: Check outside of your size on the *clearance* racks. Sometimes dresses don't sell because the manufacturer marks a size 14 with a size 8 label. I've picked up some superb dresses that way, including a recent designer style for $29 marked down from $112. Its fault? Wrong size marking. It didn't fit the size marked, so nobody bought it.

You can develop quite a lovely and diverse wardrobe this way. Of course, sometimes they sell out of your size, or whatever, before you get around to purchasing, but that's the breaks. You're playing a game, except this one can net you money if you win.

While you're working on beauty, don't pass up those fancy cosmetics. For lipstick and nail polish, check to see whether your drugstore or department store has a little wicker basket marked *close-out.* Prices are usually slashed in half, and the selection includes many brand names.

An alternative, even more fun, is checking out the current *buy one item at $8, and get a sample case of lipstick, moisturizer, eyeshadow, etc., free* offer. My biggest disappointment was getting this bonus and discovering I couldn't use the orange mascara or green lip gloss. You've got to do a bit of calculating. This may seem a bother, but then it's a bother earning those bucks, too.

Even if your budget is zilch for cosmetics at the moment, you can still try a bit of this and that while enjoying the department store offerings. I always enter looking somewhat blah, and exit rather colorful, after trying on all the products. It cheers me up so much. I just tell the salesclerks I'm testing colors, and it does save me from purchasing a pale violet blush which looks like dead plum on my cheeks.

Don't neglect the perfume garden available in test-spray bottles. A delightful fragrance makes you feel sexy, and may attract more than mosquitoes, if you're lucky. When you're buying, get the cologne instead of the more expensive concentrated perfume. You'll not only save money, but the aroma is a bit easier on the nose.

If you want the entire setup, bath powder, coordinated soap, etc., then do your cosmetics shopping right after Christmas. Most stores will do almost anything to get those wreath and Santa Claus decorated containers out of eyeshot. I do advance gift buying at this season too, selecting packages that aren't holiday garnished.

If you want a total beauty makeover, or at least a wash and set, try the local beauty schools. Some have specials on certain days, when low prices are even lower. If you are nervous about having your hair cut by a beginner, ask for an advanced student. It might cost a tad more, but nothing like what the salons charge.

In Summary

Every Monday through Friday, as a single mother, the shrilling alarm will shock you out of peaceful vacation dreams and Cinderella balls. You will shuffle children off to a babysitter or school. You will layer on clothing and trudge off to work at the factory, office, restaurant or construction site. Your pay will range from insulting to tolerable to actually fairly good.

Because you prefer not to slide any farther downward in your living standards, you will find all sorts of ingenious ways to save money. But you should still put on a bit of glitz, eat out once a month, cheer yourself up with a new trinket. Depriving yourself of these little goodies leads to feeling grumpy, put-upon, and avocado green with envy for the *haves* of this world.

You deserve the best. You work hard. You have a lot of responsibility. You are a wonderful person.

Therefore, one way or another, you will think of ways to shave the budget so you can have a bit of *splurge* cash. Do this by thinking in terms of a *shopping paycheck.* Calculate the money saved by thrifty shopping and mentally translate it into dollars earned for extra effort. Consider it a challenge. Trade secret saving schemes with equally frugal friends. Instead of frowning, happily learn from your encounters with Uncle or Aunty Scrooge. They are better than any economics professor in telling you what places offer the best bargains in town.

Silver-plated quarters do mount up into piles of wrinkled dollar bills. Try it and see. Should you develop saving skills into an art form, start taking notes. You can always write a book on *how to be super frugal in Anytown, U.S.A.* This is not only exciting, it can turn you a bit of extra profit.

This is a brand new world for you, with brand new ideas. Give new techniques a try. But leave a few bargains on the table for me, okay?

DEALING WITH DADDY

For better or worse, in sickness in health, until children do depart, or even thereafter, you will have a spouse of season's past hovering someplace over your head. This is true even if your former husband completely vanishes once the judge slams down a final gavel.

Your children will talk about Daddy from time to time. Your friends will mention "him" in guarded tones. Long-time-no-seen acquaintances will ask how your ex-husband is, either outright or sideways. Your parents and relatives will offer continual opinionated commentary. And whenever you think about your past, or look at your photo album, Eclipse will be found lingering there.

It doesn't do any good to rant and rave that you don't want to hear "that man's" name mentioned, ever. You will, 99 percent guaranteed. In many instances, unless Eclipse takes off for Mars, you may hear from him several times a week, or several times a day. This is especially true the first year or so after your divorce.

A girlfriend once steamed, "That workaholic never paid any attention to the kids while we were married. 'That's your job,' he always said. Now, presto chango, he's on the phone morning, noon and night, telling me how to improve child-care techniques, attitude, and diaper service. It's driving me nuts!"

In the initial period following a divorce, Daddy is paranoid that the physical custody Mommy will also try for full mental custody. He wants to keep his hat in at least a corner of the ring.

Your tendencies at this time lean toward a definite lack of sympathy. "If he wanted out," you think, "then out is what he gets." This is a hard line to take, and hard on the kids, too. Try to understand the motivations behind what appears to be constant criticism. Some of it may be manipulative. Other comments evidence true concern. It may be perhaps misplaced, but it does show caring.

It is best, despite verbal sparring matches tending to remind you of the marriage you just escaped from, to be grateful when Daddy shows interest. It is standard procedure, as he moves into his own separate world, for visits and phone calls to gradually decrease. In the end, expect about 25 percent of the original concern. I don't like this, because it is nice to have some backup help, but this is the consensus of opinion from my friends and my own experiences. So after you calm down a bit from the divorce blasts, try to welcome interest in whatever form it presents itself. Don't worry, or do worry. A good portion of it will be gone within a year or two.

About here some lovely lady-reader will wave an irate flag and say, "My Archibald, whatever his faults, would never neglect the kids," or "My best friend has been divorced 50 years and her ex-husband has always been 100 percent on the caring scene."

This may well be true. There are some wonderful, wonderful fathers in this world. Just because Mommy couldn't get along with Daddy, doesn't mean they both won't continue to be excellent parents. It's just that blips and blurbs occur on the most cloudless horizon from time to time. If forewarned, you can make an attempt to cope effectively.

Telephone Calls from Daddy to Mommy

There is a marked tendency, when Eclipse telephones, to use the conversation as a means of continuing century old arguments. This is not a good idea. In the first place, it raises your blood pressure. In the second place, you end up slamming down the receiver and stomping around the house, continuing the argument for the kids to hear. In the third place, even before that, while you are on the phone, they are listening, too. They are soaking in Eclipse's insane spending habits, his taste for scroungy women, his inability to resist cheap whiskey, etc.

There is a subconscious desire on your part that the children hear all about "that awful person" who once happened to be your husband and is still their father. If you stop and think about this, you may realize the harm you are doing the youngsters. It may not look like much in the short run, but in the long run, upset youngsters upset your household stability.

It won't be easy to stop snipping at Eclipse on the phone. Your fairy tale knight in shining armor has just been knocked off his silver stallion. You are very aggravated, and rightfully so, by this, but try to keep it as low key as possible when the children are around.

There are ways to make the job easier. If Daddy tends to call at a specific time of the day or evening, let the kids answer the telephone. Let them talk and talk and talk. If you can't stand what they are saying, and your blood pressure starts rising again, go into the bathroom and practice flushing. In effect, get yourself out of earshot so you won't be upset. Or at least not as annoyed as you are when overhearing the conversation.

Keep in mind that most children desperately want to have two parents. The more they realize that Daddy is gone only from the castle but not from their lives, the happier they will be. A voice on the telephone, while not as good as a warm body, fills a very genuine need. It doesn't matter what is said. It's the thought that counts. So the more casual chatting done, even about the cat, the dishes, or what Mommy said about them watching television too much, the better off the children will be.

Watch out for one unexpected glitch. You may find that while Daddy says he is calling to talk with the children, he is really calling to continue a relationship with you. Since it's easy to get *hooked* into a conversation with someone who was once an integral part of your life, you end up monopolizing the telephone time. This is true even if every conversation turns into an argument.

How do you know this is happening? Are you indulging in long personal conversations when Eclipse calls? When you try to turn the telephone over to the kids, does he suddenly have emergency business elsewhere? If this happens on even a fairly regular basis, you are hogging kid-time. Since you want to start life anew, rather than dribble on with the past, the wisest course is to jump Eclipse's conversation "hooker" before it begins.

Again, if Eclipse telephones at regular hours, let the children answer the phone. If he calls at odd times, so that you are tricked into picking up the receiver, try this scenario: "Ring. Ring." "Hello Patience. This is Eclipse. How are things going?"

Stop right there. Gird your will power. Do not lament the details of your trying day so that Eclipse knows what burdens you must deal with. Instead, sound winded. Sound like you have just completed jogging around the football field. Then say, speaking very rapidly, "Oh, I'd love to talk with you, but the bathtub is running over, the repairman is here, and the guinea pig is giving birth. Why don't you chat with one of the kids while I get everything straightened out?"

Then grab one of the toddlers, place the receiver at her/his ear, and split. Pace the hallway ten times if necessary. Walk around the block if the kid is old enough to be left alone in the house for 10 minutes.

Eclipse may still insist on talking to you afterward, but at least the children will have gotten their allotted time with Daddy. This is good for them and good for Daddy. Hearing their piping little voices assures him they are still alive and presumably well.

If you want to converse with Eclipse afterward, you can do so, depending on your current mood. If your mood is positive, what safe topics of conversation are there if the children are within earshot? Diaper rash. The latest soccer, baseball, cheerleading, frisbee, four square or hopscotch tournament. Discuss your petunias or your usual futile attempt to grow radishes indoors.

Do not get lured into an argument. Former spouses wishing to continue moribund relationships often throw in a deliberately aggravating remark to get an emotional reaction. When you find your cool starting to blow hot, get off the phone. Pretend the doorbell is ringing and hand the receiver to one of your children ... and don't come back.

If you happen to be in a bad mood, for whatever reason, and Eclipse has called umpteen times already that day or week, there is no rule you have to answer the phone at all. When Junior says, "Daddy has something very important to tell you," try the polite way out. For example, one friend turns on the shower, then hollers out, "I'm in the shower," while she reads a book or dusts.

This doesn't put Junior in the position of telling a direct lie, and also gives the impression you are a very clean person. "Listening to the shower running reminds me of a waterfall," my friend says, "which is very soothing."

It's not that you shouldn't communicate with your ex-husband. You should. They're his kids, too, even if you sometimes wished they belonged to an astronaut permanently based in outer space. But potential verbal battles are for private hours. Yell at Eclipse, if you must, when children are out of the house.

It is extremely important, after a divorce, to make every effort to turn your home back into a safe haven for the family. Everybody, including an infant, needs a place to escape from the brickbats and blowdarts the world has to offer. Since that escape mechanism in today's world tends to be the home, don't throw your own stones at the kiddies. If you do, you could do more harm than you realize.

Telephone Calls from Mommy to Daddy

This may sound unduly restrictive, but if you can avoid calling your ex-spouse (except in emergency situations) it's best to do so. Too many women use former hubby as an emotional catharsis. They telephone whenever they feel blue or out of sorts, when the car breaks down, when the plumbing goes out of plumb, when it's dark, cold and windy, or when the nights get a bit too solitary.

But who needs to hold on to a bad relationship? All you accomplish by telephoning your former spouse is a dependency continuance. And dependency is exactly what you don't want to continue.

It also doesn't improve your state of mind to call Eclipse at the office and and have his efficient secretary says she'll "see if he's in," and then you hear her business-like voice, followed by his business-like voice, after which she informs you—very business-like—that Eclipse is "out of town," "out to lunch," "out to the Casbah," and can she take a message?

If that situation makes you instantly feel like a contagious disease, wait until you try calling Eclipse at home. Now his current girlfriend, mistress or even boyfriend may answer the phone. It is a statistical fact that men tend to take up with a roommate a lot faster than women with children. How fast will probably amaze you, since you probably at least expect the marriage will be given a decent burial and mourning period.

There's even a good chance Vampira will be the one to answer the telephone. She will yawn obviously and sigh, "I'll go see if Eclipse can come to the phone." Even if you telephoned in a calm, collected state of mind, it goes out the window as you wait and wait.

When Eclipse finally does meander over, his greeting may be something like, "What do you want?" As if you were a bill collector or an annoying third cousin trying to borrow a buck. So you tell him what you want. You know all the while that Vampira is tapping her bare feet within earshot of the phone. Who needs it? Certainly not you. You're trying to get better, not rip open old wounds.

Should you have an emergency message, and few actually are—give it some thought, then by all means convey the message—briefly. However, if it concerns anything less significant than a child going to the hospital, count ten and <u>don't</u> dial.

Clean the oven, wax the floors, scrub the sink with a toothbrush, but figure out a way to cope all by your lonesome. When you need to hear a reassuring voice, call that girlfriend who never lets you get a word in edge-wise. After you finish with that conversation, you won't want to talk to anybody for hours. This will get you through the *bad* period, and hopefully your out-of-sorts will have sorted itself out.

Even if Eclipse is one of those former husbands who run to the phone dutifully every time you call, and can discuss noncommittal things like how to repair an exhaust pipe, you still don't want to start the ball rolling. Ex-husbands can also get caught up in the same emotional catharsis game you're playing. Neither of you may realize it is a game, and a losing game at that.

The end of a marriage presents an opportunity to take a good, hard, mature look at yourself. How do you deal with crisis, periods of emptiness, the people around you at work or in the neighborhood? If you use your ex-husband as a crutch, it just takes that much longer to figure out how to climb that mountain of a molehill by yourself.

The next time you're tempted to dial D-A-D-D-Y, ask yourself what you would do if he was an astronaut circling the moon. Then go ahead and try to solve the problem yourself. Your methods may be rusty, halt and hesitant. That's o.k. You will more often find that what looks difficult truly isn't, and you are a much more capable person than you thought.

I remember when my lemon of a car stopped dead in an employment agency parking lot. Automobile problems have always sent me into total panic, so I rushed to the phone to call my ex-husband. He always took care of *that* type of thing. I picked up the receiver, put it down. I picked it up again, dialed, put it down. I picked it up, let it ring once, slammed it down.

My ex-husband would have solved the problem by telling me to call the auto service. After this advice, I would have called the auto service. So why couldn't I bypass one step? I could. I did. The car got fixed. No big deal. I came out feeling very capable.

You too can learn to shut off the water supply at home, smoosh a gopher, and change the plug on a lamp. And if you ever get to the point, and you probably will, where you can install an overhead light fixture, fix a plumbing snafu, and repair a screen door, then you know the feeling of true genius that comes from a "do-it-yourself" success.

So in times of trouble, don't dial D-A-D-D-Y, dial S-E-L-F S-U-F-F-I-C-I-E-N-C-Y. It may take a little longer, but on a cold night you will feel ever so much warmer inside.

Child Support

Getting your court-ordered child support can involve such aggravation that many women give up trying. Others say, "I don't want anything from that b__. The less I hear from him the better, even if it means going without."

Yet if you deliberately decide not to go after the dollars which mean the difference between miserable times and just plain hard times, you'll live to regret it; you'll regret it now, 10 years from now, and 20 years from now.

"I raised five kids all by my lonesome," Stalwart Annie says once again. "Their father never sent them a dime (notice the message), but they turned out just fine (heroine image)."

Yes, Annie's kids did turn out just fine. She has good reason to be proud. But given any opportunity to collect child support, you should go after it hammer and claw, tooth and nail.

When I got discouraged about this, I went to a friend who could be counted at to yell at me for slothfulness. Everybody needs at least one of these feisty folk to get them going again when they're ready to quit.

Sarah called me a coward. She said I had "no guts." She asked me if I didn't think my children deserved the best. She said, "For them you have to do it. Not for you." And when my perspective was verbally bullied back into sensible shape, I set my aim on better results and got them with the extra effort.

If your former spouse has a fixed-location employment address, guerrilla tactics might include sending him postcards with big block lettering stating, "Child support is overdue again." Other messages that have been used effectively include, "This is your friendly ex-wife inquiring about late child support payments," or "Please pay child support promptly so I can keep a roof over your children's heads." Since few ex-hubbies like the idea of postcards with snitty commentary being read by the postman, town clerk, and secretarial gossips, such *public* notices sometimes help.

Should Eclipse be the type who carries the child support check in his pocket for weeks, pleading lack of time to go to the post office for a stamp, send him a self-addressed stamped envelope prior to the due date.

If this doesn't get results, perhaps putting you in a fiscal emergency situation, call his office. You don't particularly want to talk to Eclipse. His excuses for late payment can be taped once on a recorder and played back forever. They never vary. So, leave a message with his answering service, secretary, or whichever co-worker picks up the phone. "The kids are hungry. I just bounced a check due to insufficient funds. Do you think you could remind Eclipse to give me a little of the overdue child support payment to help with the groceries and the heating bill."

The whole situation is the pits. You may have to go farther than second-hand messages. I have one acquaintance who makes a once-a-month pilgrimage to her ex-spouse's manufacturing plant. Here she sits in the lobby with a large placard stating, "Please pay my child support, Joe Eclipse. The landlord is threatening to evict us." Unusual perhaps. But in this situation, it is effective where nothing else works.

Should your ex-spouse be out of sight but not quite out of mind, consult an attorney. Some legal aid societies will help if you're broke, although government funding cuts have made these worthy groups overburdened and understaffed. Laws vary from state to state, but many have some type of enforcement provisions. When Eclipse gets a formal note, written on letterhead paper, he knows you're serious. Otherwise he assumes you are issuing your usual weak threats.

The worst situations come when former spouse gets a substantial proportion of his income in cash. Lila's ex-husband did plumbing "on the side." Although he always had enough money for ski trips and assorted holidays, when tax time came around there was never enough documented inflow to require filling out a tax form. Lila hauled him into court on multiple occasions. But Eclipse always pleaded the most dire poverty. Lila had no way of proving otherwise, short of hiring an expensive private detective to follow him about.

Similar problems can occur when Eclipse owns his own business. He then controls the bookwork which makes it appear that incoming assets are minimal. In this situation, however, you may be able to place a sheriff or *keeper* in his office to garnish monies as they come in. It's a real hassle, but if he's in a business where embarrassment must be kept to a minimum, a *keeper* only has to show up once for checks to start flowing with more regularity.

If you had known what you were in for, which most women going through a divorce either do not know or else are too emotionally distraught to consider, there are some preventive measures smart ladies can employ. During divorce negotiations, see if you can get child support payments taken directly from his paycheck and mailed to you. For various reasons, Eclipse may consent to this. Some men hate to ink a child support check, and prefer to have the monies just disappear at home plate. This route eliminates a lot of hassles. It's worth trying for.

Another way of collecting is through your county district attorney's office. They may have a child support division. It is overloaded, understaffed, underfunded, etc., but it works. I know, I've been there.

You may be able to get your ex-spouse to agree to this peaceably. If not, you may have to document that he is a continual late or non-payer. You can do this by photocopying your child support checks from Day One following your divorce instigation, and the front of the envelope they came in—showing the postmarked mailing date. You'll need to confirm the postmark because some ex-spouses will date a check June 1 and mail it July 31. (I used to joke about getting paid promptly on the forty-third of each month.) The date and postmark on the envelope tells the child support system, or any attorney you might use, that the checks are late.

If you go via the state collection system, be aware that it might take as long as a year to get through. Should you need a little muscle to move it, try calling your local legislator. Sometimes a phone call from an assemblyperson's secretary, or congressman's secretary, can do wonders.

As a note, you do not have to be a welfare mother to use the district attorney's office to collect child support. Nor should you believe your attorney when he says it doesn't work. That's what my attorneys kept saying. What this did was keep me running to them—at $150 an hour. It wasn't until I talked to a bank manager and mentioned collection problems, that she told me about using the district attorney's office to collect from her spouse, also a bank manager. Mandated payments are for any income bracket. Basically the child support agency collects for you, then mails you their check—which won't bounce like a rubber ball.

What if none of these approaches work—for various reasons, and Eclipse is supposed to be sending you X dollars monthly, but nothing gets it out of him, or he's broke or just plain vanished? Make certain, regardless of how little you figure he'll ever have, to get a child support judgment. Even $50 a month mounts over time. If he pays you anything, photocopy the check and envelope. If he doesn't, keep track of how much is owed. Then try to keep track of Eclipse. If he owns a house, you can put a child support lien on it. That means he can't sell the house until he pays you. One gal collected every single dime owed for 15 years this way. Her ex-husband inherited a home from his mother. When he tried to sell it, bingo!

I've also heard about children being able to sue delinquent parents as adults, collecting the monies long overdue for college expenses. It's worth checking out.

Whatever method you use, it helps to have a competent attorney. Remember that competence costs as much as incompetence, and sometimes less. It pays to shop around. Ask everybody and their aunt which attorney they used, the attorney's attitude, procedures utilized, etc.

My first attorney was male. My second attorney was a male. My third was a female. My fourth was a female. One was competent, one quasi-competent, and two I considered robbers.

My best advice is to learn as much divorce law as you possibly can. Read everything, particularly current law. (Nolo Press in Berkeley, California has some excellent reasonably priced books.) You don't have to handle your own divorce, but for your own sake you should know what's going on in the courtroom.

Attorneys give you extravagant promises as to what can be collected. "There, there, now. We'll take care of that mean man. Just leave it to me." The only thing you might collect are extravagant promises, and you'll pay dearly for those. When push comes to shove, and the attorney figures he or she has gotten as much out of you as possible, you'll soon hear, "We may have to settle for a reasonable sum." Of course, this is a lot less than you were originally told. However the whole thing has dragged on so long, you've reached the point where you're glad to get anything. In most instances, Eclipse comes out the winner, although he grumps and grumbles. Studies show his disposable income rises 40 percent or more. Yours drops at least that much.

Whichever attorney you choose, get one who specializes in divorce and its aftermath. You don't want somebody who takes a quickie divorce case amidst corporate cases. You will find yourself last on a list of things to do. Your paltry deposit, which isn't paltry to you, is small on an agenda which includes huge business retainers or thousands of dollars in prospective fees. Nor should you hesitate, after a few years have passed, to go back into the courtroom. Most women hate to do this. They take the same piddling sum granted when their child is one-year-old, and make it do until the little one turns eighteen. In the meantime, Eclipse has progressed up the economic ladder and is now making $45,000 a year instead of $22,000.

Women are afraid the judge will lower their child support. I've never heard of this actually being done, although anything is possible. At worst, it will be left the same. Mostly, today's courts consider the cost of living index and are inclined to raise child support if you persist in asking that this be done. They are, after all, Eclipse's children too, whether he chooses to enjoy them fully or not.

However it is up to you to make certain that Eclipse knows that monies received go toward child-care expenses. If he sees rags on the kids and booze on the shelf, as does happen, there's lots of motivation for him to not want to increase child support payments. And some men use rags and booze as an excuse for not paying at all.

And how does Eclipse know where the cash is going? Seeing is believing. Regular communication helps if vision is obscured by distance. Tell Eclipse if you have taken the kids out to buy new slacks and shirts. Better yet, have the kids tell him. Talk about the numerous requests you get from the school for field trip contributions and gym clothes. Send him receipts if you have to. Throw in a tidbit concerning the rise in babysitter's rates. Mention the doubling of auto insurance for your teenaged driver. And don't forget those dental and doctor's visits that eat up the gas budget.

Eclipse may shrug, or he may counter with his own living expenses, but the message usually filters through after a while. Absentee fathers often lose touch with how much it costs to rear a child. They're not around to see the small and large items that munch away at your wallet. So, you must tell them. Don't gripe, just pass on the facts.

Raising kids is a hard job and it costs money. If Eclipse had to pay a babysitter $1.50 or more an hour, that would be $15 a working day, $450 a month. And that doesn't include babysitting time during non-work hours.

When I took my first paid-sitter vacation, local agencies wanted $50 a day *if* they could "get anybody to take on four children." And that was quite a while ago. Now it is easily double.

Eclipse is really getting a bargain in your services, which also include more personal interest than is available from any babysitter. It is quite reasonable to expect him to pay the child support dole on time, plus give regular cost-of-living increases. If you can get this message across somehow, it really does help balance your meager budget.

Daddy's assistance with the budget balancing act also truly helps cut down constant gripes like, "Your father doesn't give a dime," and "Your father has enough to support his girlfriend/new wife/boyfriend in style. But you should see what a teeny bit he gives me for you." Commentary of this order, no matter how offhand, is bad for the children's sense of self-worth. It creates even more problems for you to handle, and who needs that?

If you think of the child support payments in the same light as you would a paycheck, you'll go after them in a businesslike and persistent manner. You are, after all, just getting paid for a job.

The Other Woman in His Life

As mentioned, Eclipse will probably find a live-in love much faster then you will. This may be a casual series of persons, a glued-to-him mistress, a new wife, a series of new wives, or—that modern phenomenon—a series of new gentleman friends. The latter are beyond the expertise of this author, so lets just deal with the ladies.

You will not jump for joy on hearing of whomever replaces you. And your attitude will be decidedly negative if Eclipse decides to make her legal. When a former spouse remarries, women go into quite a depression. This is true even though they have been divorced for ages. While you wouldn't have Eclipse return if he was dipped in gold, you still hurt. There is no logical explanation for this, so just accept it.

If his new wife was part of your pre-divorce aggravation, you will also experience an increase in tension in your relations with Eclipse. Even if Vampira didn't meet Eclipse until 10 years after the divorce, you probably will not welcome her arrival with open arms.

Vampira's presence means added expenses for Eclipse, and less freed up money for the children of a prior marriage. A new wife means someone who wants to spend time with him, her way, and this adds up to less time for his previous family. It also may mean a new family. The idea of children being with him every day, instead of alternate Sundays, will upset your children as much, or more, than it upsets you.

Still, Vampira is there. Eclipse is entitled to resume his life. You are going to have to adjust. How well you do this depends on how well you set up emotional and household rules. These rules must be realistic, even though emotionally you can expect to falter every so often.

The basic rule is, "Get out of their life." Many women claim to have an absolutely marvelous relationship with wife #2, #3 or #4. They may even meet for cocktails once in a while. But closer examination shows specks on the communal flypaper. What you're actually doing is continuing a relationship with Eclipse. After all, who else do you talk about in those friendly little chats?

For example, Eclipse and Vampira are having a spat. She may make a remark on one of his wee habits, like cutting his toenails in bed. Can you truly resist adding your two-cents-worth? Haven't you a hundred stories to top the toenail anecdote? So you share a few chuckles. A few hours later, Vampira shares your stories with Eclipse. He does not chuckle. Instead, Vampira and Eclipse get into an argument. This does not abet their wedded bliss, and may lend to its demise.

You, despite private thoughts, gain no benefit from this. Even if you get rid of her, Eclipse will no doubt soon take up with another female. She might not be better than Vampira, and she may be worse. And, the more relationships he has, the greater the chance of more babies. The more babies, the more lawyers (paternity suits and/or new divorces) he will pay. The more lawyers he will pay, the more erratic he will get. The more erratic he gets, the more aggravation you get. So why bother? With all the women in this world, there must be a few you can chat with besides Eclipse's new wives.

Keep communication with Vampira brief and businesslike. When you telephone, it's not necessary to engage in a round of social chatter. Just say, "Hello Vampira. This is Patience. Can I please talk to Eclipse?" If you have an emergency message regarding the children, then deliver that message to Eclipse. If he's not home, just say, "One of the children is turning bright green. Can Eclipse call me when he gets home?" Then say good-bye and hang up; there's usually no problem with Vampira forwarding your request.

Of course, Vampira may be reluctant to relay your message if you're one of those ex-wives that call on any possible pretext, or if you keep Eclipse on the phone for hours, dumping your blues or sharing remembrances. This is a rank invasion of their home life. You are not entitled, based on your prior relationship, to make anything more than a cameo appearance in Eclipse's present life.

What if Eclipse seems to welcome your soliloquies? Suppose he tells Vampira to send up flares whenever you telephone? Consider this scene some years from now, when you've perhaps found a new mate. Will you like it when Eclipse calls and expects you to listen to his problems? Your present mate won't like it either. Stop this potential ping-pong game before it starts. You have a new life. Eclipse has a new life. Welcome the rebirth, labor contractions and all.

Another good rule is to try not to spend your time systematically poisoning the children's minds against Daddy's new wife. This works in the short run, but can smash back in the long run.

I remember Celia's story. It seems Daddy took off with a gal much his junior. This left Mommy very bitter. She objected when Celia talked to the new wife. Daddy objected to the way Celia soon learned to talk to the new wife. After multiple arguments on the subject, all communication between father and daughter ceased.

Celia, torn two ways, felt she hadn't much choice on how to behave. Perhaps she didn't, given Mommy's continual broken heart and constant reminders of who broke it. But when Daddy died of a heart attack, something went *boing*. Celia got to thinking that he may not have been such a bad guy after all. She recalled how he built her that lovely little dollhouse once upon a time, and helped her with her schoolwork even when he was tired. She felt like cow apples, guilty and unable to undo the damage. After an extended series of crying jags followed by counseling sessions, Celia decided the guilt wasn't all hers. Now Mommy and Celia don't talk to each other very much.

Nobody wins this game. Children don't have to love Vampira. They don't even have to like her. Like and love are earned. But children must learn to be cordial, saying "please" and "thank you." They should also ask Vampira how *she's* doing, from time to time. If you block basic manners by running off at the mouth about Vampira's background, personal characteristics, and whooping lifestyle, you are blocking the free flow of communication with Daddy. You do not want to do this. All children want a father, and they have one—your ex-husband, remarried or not.

Try to cut out the verbal poison even if Vampira isn't a wife, but is instead a mistress or revolving live-in. Be polite. That's all that's needed. Yes, sometimes Eclipse gets carried away insisting the children adore his current companion. That is so complex a maneuver, don't even try to reason with it. Usually he will cool it after a while. So hang in there, and encourage the kids to be cordial, the same way they are to the postman, grocery clerk, school crossing guard and the local harmless eccentric. If you think of *other*-family communication as a lesson in manners, your children will definitely benefit and carry the manners into other situations.

There is also a chance that the children will actually like Vampira. This can be very hard on your ego. She may cook superb brownies, tell original bedtime stories, and be super loving and kind, and all this will be reported to you in detail each time the children visit. Even on days when everything else seems to be plotting against you, try to force a lopsided grin and bear it.

Tell yourself over and over again how lucky you are that Daddy married such a wonderful woman. How pleased you are that she is so nice to the kids. Remind yourself that if Vampira is a super person, you don't have to worry about the children when they visit her and Daddy, which is actually true.

If Vampira likes your children, she will have them visit often. Even if she doesn't actually adore the youngsters, but merely wants to be a good wife to Eclipse, she will have the children visit and they will have a nice time. This gives you, looking from the bright side, free babysitting. It also gives you time to take an uninterrupted bubblebath, invite your beau over, or go on a no deadline shopping excursion.

If Vampira truly enjoys the youngsters, she may even welcome their grubby little bodies over to her place for a week or two while you vacation. This is worth its weight in gold, with sitters costing premium prices and not always being very reliable or caring.

It requires some very deliberate emotional balancing to accept this "really great person" who appears to threaten your supermom position, even though she doesn't.

You will always and forever be "Mother" to your children. No one will ever take your place in their hearts. So relax and enjoy. Not all single mother's are lucky enough to have a willing caretaker for the youngsters, who just happens to be married to Daddy.

ARE EX-IN-LAWS OUTLAWS?

Your mother-in-law has never really liked you. Now is your chance to bow out of the family yo-yo match. No longer do you have to listen to unwanted advice, go anyplace for holiday dinners besides home, or feel like a second wheel. For many women, the departure of in-laws is one of the brightest glimmers in the storm clouds that hover over a divorce. At least so it seems, at first.

Later you realize that when the judge sets aside umpteen years of marital disharmony, you have not only lost a spouse, you also tend to lose the entire web of family connections from his side. Aunts, uncles, cousins, sisters-in-law, etc., just seem to disappear.

Some former relatives will not talk to you after they hear of your separation. You have somehow instantly been transformed into a simpleminded, spendthrift, nymphomaniac. Your very words place a hex on their bunions.

Other former kinfolk will telephone once or twice. They will offer opinions on your *hasty* actions. They will probably be offended when you slam down the phone, and not offer free counseling again. They will also not offer any other type of aid.

There is also a third group. These few are the generally kind-hearted souls, often the ones the entire family takes advantage of. These people will continue an occasional communication and pass the message of your continued existence. Former kinfolk may not want anything to do with you, but human nature being what it is, they will inquire amongst themselves if you are still in the land of the living.

A fourth group does exist. Over the years you may have established a personal bond with a kinfolk member. They will like you just the same as ever, but they may not speak up at first. Penalties for siding with the enemy camp can be quite severe.

So, suddenly, you turn from the divorce court and half a family seems to have disappeared. This may not be apparent initially. It will dawn on you a bit later, when you do not get invited to a wedding, a funeral, or a christening. Instead, you hear about these kinfolk activities about six months later, in a roundabout way.

Along comes Christmas, Easter and Thanksgiving. You are accustomed to sitting down at a table laden for sixteen persons. Only now it's different. If your own family is small, as mine is, or if they live in Big Apple while you reside in Little Peach, you suddenly find yourself staring at a turkey hindquarters and a few canned sweet potatoes.

You begin to miss the familial color of the holidays. It's not that you really miss cheek-pinching Uncle Joe or whiny-voiced Cousin Clara. However, surely you can share a homemade apple dumpling with jovial Aunt Annabelle. Can't you?

How well you have gotten along with Eclipse's relatives prior to your divorce often determines how well you get along with them afterwards. But it does take time for slung mud to settle, so even the best of kinfolk relationships take a while to resume sometimes. When they do start up again, you often have to take the first step.

Why should you bother? After all, they accept Eclipse with all his faults, and never were overly friendly to you. The rationale for trying to resume kinfolk relationships is akin to what Alex Haley called "roots." Not yours; you know what they are. However, your children need roots on both sides of the family. It helps them to grow.

Family, unless harmfully looney, is good for kids. Family provides children with a sense of stability, a feeling of belonging somewhere. This is extremely important in a world where neighbors are transferred to new jobs overnight, and Mommy sometimes seems a bit shell shocked from holding down the home fortress single-handed.

But what approach can you take, given this divided camp? If your offspring are old enough to clutch a crayon, the opening gambit can be theirs with a fanciful sketch. They can make their name sign on the sketch. You address the envelopes.

School age youngsters can write "How are you? I am fine. I had fun in class today." The first few letters might not produce results. But keep them flowing. Eventually the more sociable, family oriented, or softhearted kinfolk will send a little note back. Ex-in-laws may be waging war with you, but if the children are clever enough to write, it will be assumed that they obviously take after Eclipse's side of the family.

Keep your hot little hands off the initial phases of correspondence. Let the renewed relationship mellow a bit. After a while you can start penning postscripts to the children's letters. But keep off the subject of your own well-being and stick to the subject of little Priscilla or Percy.

For example, you might add on, "Percy hit his first home run today," or "Percy and Priscilla are now singing soprano in the church choir." Keep your messages short and sweet. Don't mention the kids current shoplifting escapades, or how Priscilla stuck a bean up her nose. Such negative notes tend to be interpreted as a direct swipe against Eclipse for having left his defenseless children to cope without a father figure. Relatives don't like to hear that type of slur on the family tree, true or not. Keep your writing touch light, positive, and as cheerful as possible. It will be appreciated.

You may be tempted, however, when jovial Aunt Annabelle sends you a really long letter, to pour out your heart in response. After all, she should know that Eclipse forgot to send his child support for the zillionth time. Not only that, but Percy needs expensive braces and you can't pay for them. All this is terribly hard on your uterus, hernia, and/or fallen arches, but don't whine on paper to Eclipse's family. Save the problems for your own side of the family. They don't mind, and it makes them feel better about their own difficulties anyhow.

Aunt Annabelle may be very jovial, but she used to bounce Eclipse on her knee. Your heart-rending commentary merely puts a cramp in her writing hand. This may be the same hand she stirs the apple dumplings with, so be gentle.

And keep in mind that humorous sarcasm is not acceptable. Once I asked my girlfriend, Rosemary, whether she ever heard from her ex-in-laws. "Well," she replied, "we started out by exchanging greeting cards. Then we rapidly progressed to polite little letters. It seemed, after a while, our correspondence was becoming more substance than fluff. But then came Christmas, and I got in one of my moods. So I added this postscript to the card. 'You'll be pleased to know that Rob enjoys his girlfriend's company even more now that he's single.' I haven't heard another word from my ex-in-laws since then," Rosemary concluded. "Not one of them. I guess the word got around."

Now suppose you have zippered your lip appropriately. All is apparently going smoothly. You are now ready to initiate a face-to-face meeting, using the children as a shoehorn. In your letters, casually mention something like, "Percy would really enjoy seeing Uncle Rudolph's train/C.B. radio/stamp collection," or "Priscilla would really like to learn how to cook pretzels/bread/stuffed cabbage, the way you do, Aunt Tillie. If you have some time to teach her, it would really be appreciated."

Eventually, if you cajole long enough, you may receive an invitation to visit from Aunt Tillie or Uncle Rudolph's wife. But now you have to pass over another hurdle. You can always tear up a letter. Sitting in someone's living room you cannot take words back.

Whatever wariness applies to correspondence applies quadruple to personal socialization. Stick to talk about the kids, home decorating, the dog, or your job. While this sounds easy, it isn't.

For example, what happens when you're asked how you are doing on the social scene? Still smarting from Eclipse's having vanished with Vampira, you may be tempted to boast of your prowess in collecting males, even if you are not dating at all.

Don't boast. Every word you say, punctuated with colorful adjectives for added interest, will get passed along the family pipeline. Eclipse, after hearing the news that his ex-wife is making the bar scene every night and bringing the dregs home, will become irate. That message is a lie; you've met a few fellows at church socials, but that's all. And you never bring them home. How did that get translated into a wild evening of sadomasochism in your living room?

It's a lot like a child's game of *Telephone*. Remember: We all sat around in a circle. Someone started a sentence, and whispered into the ear of the adjoining person. The sentence was then passed around the room. It was truly amazing how much the sentence had changed by the end of the game.

While you are not really worried anymore about what Eclipse thinks about anything, it's best not to rile him with unnecessary irritations. If you think child support payments are late now, wait until they're sent via Timbuktu. Late child support payments are often used to punish former wives. So do your own thing, but there's no necessity for throwing it out for all the relatives to see.

Still, that doesn't answer the question, "How *are* you doing on the social scene?"

Before the silence becomes unbearable, you might respond vaguely, "Oh, I get out a bit. But I always feel I should spend my time with the children." Are you lying? Gee, depending on what you want it to mean, that response can be translated as "I get out a bit to group orgies. But when I sober up, I always feel like I would have been better off with the brats."

Yes, that's silly. But you get the drift. If you haven't said you're indulging in anything remotely wicked, nobody knows and you haven't lied either. Keeping track of outright falsehoods is a nuisance, especially as they begin accumulating and you forget who told what to whom.

It's also best not to boast about your paycheck. In a few years you may be taking Eclipse back to court for a child support increase. You don't want him to tell the judge that you're raking in $36 million a week. It sounds like you don't need a nickle more.

When pinned to the wall with, "What's your salary?" many ladies, skilled in evasive techniques, give their take-home net. In translation, that's your paycheck without mentioning the standard deductions for taxes, pension fund, medical, dental, social security, stock options, bond plans, etc.

Since the amount you take home is usually at least a third less than what you actually earn, you have reduced your salary considerably. Nor are you fibbing. You are just shading your answer a bit, as "We manage to live quite comfortably on $8,000 a year."

You will also be asked about Eclipse's social life. The question may be delicately phrased, such as "Do you know if Eclipse has found anyone of interest?" or less delicately phrased, such as "What do you think of Eclipse's old/new girlfriend. The one with her neckline down to her kneecaps?"

Don't let your killer instinct resurface. If you do, you'll say something like, "Oh, Eclipse has found a batch of groupies at his intellectual level. You know, third grade," or "Eclipse is living with some gal who just graduated from a halfway house."

This may satisfy your need for fanged revenge, and your former kinfolk's need for juicy scandal, but in the long run it's still Eclipse's family. They won't like you for the insult. Somehow it implies a genetic weakness surging through the genealogical tree.

Pass the buck by saying, "Eclipse and I don't talk about his social life," or "Eclipse seems reasonably content with his new lifestyle," or even "Eclipse's girlfriend (not *mistress*) is just what he needs at this time." You can always say, if queried further, that you don't talk about the children's father when they might be listening at the keyhole. Nobody will fault you for this. Most will, even if disappointed, respect you instead.

All the above caution must be quintupled if your meeting is with your former mother or father-in-law. They have a vested interest in Eclipse's well-being. It makes no difference whether he has been an absolutely rotten child, disrespectful, inattentive and consistently mocking. Your in-laws still diapered, burped and potty trained him. In addition, he's got Daddy's hairline and Momma's chin. They will be on his side 100 percent. Accept it, and go on from there.

Keep in mind that these people are your children's grandparents, and you can overcome most communication obstacles. They know, and you know, that half of Percy and Priscilla's genes come from Eclipse's side of the family. This makes the kids their lifeline to posterity. This lifeline can bridge many a dislike, including their possible dislike of you.

If you have never, ever, liked your in-laws, it's not easy to put forth the extra effort that communication entails. But as you sow, so shall you reap. Children who see you treat the older generation with courtesy will have ample example for treating you similarly when it's your turn to be grey-haired and a bit tired.

Frankly, I got along much better with my mother-in-law after my divorce than I ever did during my marriage. During my marriage, I always felt that my carpeting was the wrong color, my hair went to the wrong beautician, my kids ate the wrong food, and my treatment of her wonderful son could markedly improve.

Surprisingly, problems seemed to disappear when Eclipse went back on the open market. Suddenly I became a paragon of virtue. Not immediately, of course, but after Grandma got a bird's-eye view of possible succeeding alternatives to yours truly, my status markedly improved.

Now Grandma and I sit and chat like old friends, which we are. We have a lot in common, the kids, a need to keep family together, plus many years interaction with each other's warts and assorted pains. We don't discuss my dating life. We don't discuss her son's social life. Nor do we discuss finances, although many times it is tempting.

No matter what blame you would like to lay on your in-laws for Eclipse's dastardly upbringing, what's done is done, and cannot be re-done. Your in-laws did the best they could, given lifestyle circumstances and their own upbringing. There are also many other facets shaping a youngster's life besides parents. As your own children grow older, you will become much more sympathetic. Some factors are really not under parental control.

If you still don't like your in-laws, hopefully, unless they're really looney tunes and destructive, you can learn to tolerate them for the sake of the children. After all, given your busy schedule, there isn't that much time to see anybody that often. But you and the children should still visit once in a while, or have your in-laws visit you.

If Grandma or Grandpa get on your nerves during the visit, excuse yourself to go grocery shopping or walk the cat. Come back in half an hour. Sometimes your absence is the best thing for grandparents and grandchildren. Grownups tend to talk to each other, excluding the younger set. When you stop running interference, the senior generation gets to know the little ones a lot better. And if encouraged, even the shiest child will find something to say.

There is one little misery connected to all this which you should be prepared for. After their grandparents depart, the children tend to repeat selected portions of their conversation. "Grandpa says we look skinny. He wants to know if we're eating the right foods," or "Grandma thinks we're a bit nervous. Are we getting enough sleep?"

Youngsters of divorced families seem to like to try out their mother's reactions to aggravation. Unless you're prepared, you may just shoot from the hip with a comment about Eclipse's mental diseases being inherited from those same mean-mouthed people who are telling you how to raise your family.

To the children, this is family insight, which they store away, perhaps bringing it up 100 years in the future. If you didn't say anything, they'd forget the remarks. Actually, they're probably repeating half of them incorrectly and totally out of context, just as they do when they tattle on their siblings. So be prepared and keep your cool.

If you are continually on the receiving end of helpful hints from your in-laws, stop and listen. They may actually be seeing something that you don't, and the hints can be helpful. Older people do tend to have more practical experience, and as a single working mother, you are sometimes so exhausted you don't see the forest for the trees.

If *helpful hints* become annoying, you can counter by saying, "The children and I try not to dwell on your few weak points. It would be nice if you wouldn't dwell on my few weak points either."

You may have to say this multiple times in various ways, but eventually your polite message should make it past hearing aids and into memory. If not, try to bounce the critiques off by jogging, racewalking, or shadowboxing, all of which are good for your health and soothe the mood.

Here's another item for your *be prepared* list. As children mature from baby talk to the blab stage, they also tend to make remarks which would be better left unsaid. For example, if you returned home just once at 4:00 a.m., acting rather silly due to a

few extra sips of fresh air, children can make it seem like y
all the time. Or if you sideswiped a parked car because you had
other things on your mind that day, the children can make it seem
like you regularly drive in a demolition derby.

Constantly remind Percy and Priscilla that they should keep
their mouths shut regarding your personal life. Under no circumstances are they to talk about you at all to your ex-in-laws. With a
little prompting, kids can become very adept at zipping their lips.
And their reward is a peaceful mother, which is nice following the
loudness of a divorce.

Sometimes you have to lay it on the line directly. Mention that
if Percy or Priscilla keep mentioning Momma's foibles to Daddy's
parents, you will mention to their best friend that they wet the bed
until they were five, or sucked their thumb until they were nine.
With the *mentions* on the other foot, youngsters can become mar-
velously sympathetic to your cause.

Still, you must give children something to talk about. This
takes some advance preparation. Practice "Tell Grandpa about
your 'A' in basket weaving," or "Tell Grandma how you got your
Boy Scout merit badge in knot tying."

Go over, in advance, a list of items that grandparents like to
hear about. These include cookie baking, school art projects, books
read, field trips, and helping Mommy paint the kitchen. Then
encourage the youngsters to ask about when Grandma and
Grandpa were little. This gambit usually prompts quite a bit of
storytelling, which everybody enjoys.

All this seems like a lot of effort. But if you can grin and bear
it, the children will get along with their grandparents a lot better.
If they do, the in-law grandparents will tolerate you a lot better. If
you truly get lucky, they may even offer to take the children off
your hands for a few days, enabling you to run off to the Casbah
for a few days—or at least go walking on the beach. It's a vacation
you can take peacefully, knowing that you have kept okay people
on your peace list.

Think family. Write holiday cards to your ex-kinfolk. Have the
children write, call, and visit. It always helps to know there's an
extra port when life holds the possibility of a storm.

DATES, PLUMS, AND FIGS

Whatever happened to the goodnight kiss? The kind where you stood on tiptoes under the porch light, puckered up, closed your eyes, waited for him to remove his glasses, and then, whammo, hot diggety-dog, that light brush of soft lips.

The thrill hit your knees, bounced someplace around the kidneys, then settled solidly near the wilting orchid corsage pinned to your coat. Quick now, through the door where Momma stood sleepy-eyed. Then to bed, with dreams composed of sheer fantasy.

The evening had been perfect. You were the fairy princess transformed from a scullery maid. The aura would last maybe an entire week, until, should you ever be so lucky, shining knight would call again.

The nostalgic notion is enough to make a veteran of today's skirmishes sigh. When did it change? Perhaps it was the starry post-divorce night I puckered up, and instead of a light brush of lips, found myself trying to cope with a damp tongue being forcefully thrust between clenched teeth.

Whazzat? Everybody's doing it. Well, I don't like it. Don't be such a stick in the mud. So maybe I am. You betcha. Bye ....

The initials the fellows used were P.T. I remember I had to ask, in complete confidence, whispering to my friend, what that stood for. "Prick tease," she whispered back, looking around to make certain she wasn't overheard.

Was that me? Were the baggy sweaters and calf-length skirts I wore issuing an invitation to some pimply male that I was prepared to carry through? Was I one of *those?*

The years flew by and gradually, through accumulated encounters, I figured out which end was up—and it usually was. Coming to the door of my quaint little abode, where Momma was no longer waiting with ear to keyhole, the closed-eye pucker became the furthest thing from my mind.

Should I let him in? Damn, I was tired, had become a pumpkin at the stroke of twelve, and it was already 3:00 a.m. But Lochinvar was prepped for action, and I still hadn't made up my mind whether he was Prince Charming or a frog in disguise. But it was expected. Everybody was doing it. Didn't I read current magazines? Couldn't I take a rain check? See you on the street car. They don't run anymore. I know.

Tripping Over Your Ego

My girlfriend, formerly a staid housewife and just recently into the single's scenario, just announced that she had selected three bachelors from work headquarters and invited them to her apartment for tea and sympathy. "I got laid on Friday, Saturday, and Sunday nights," she announced proudly, as she also scanned my face for any hint of condemnation.

I raised not an eyebrow. There was no hint of scorn. I had heard the story before.

For the first year or two following a divorce, women have a tremendous need to verify their status as attractive desirable females. Divorce is not only an emotional battering ram, it is an insult to a woman's sexual self-image. This is especially true if Eclipse has been inattentive, impotent, or unfaithful.

Depending on how conservative or liberal an upbringing she had, Ms. Newly Single will be doing the town in various shades of enthusiasm. Single's dances, single's bars, single's clubs, encounter groups, and *let-it-all-hang-out* organizations all comprise the initial hunting ground for the perfect male. The next round is surely going to be a lot better than the first one with Eclipse.

If your ego is dashed to smithereens and hanging together with paste when you start this routine, you haven't seen anything yet. You've lost 10 pounds, done the health spa bit, dyed your hair blonde, buttoned up your I.Q., and figure you're a worthwhile asset to anyone's portfolio.

However, during your initial frantic period, you're more likely to find guys interested solely in wildcat stocks, purchased for a penny a share and ready for sale tomorrow. Eventually, you will probably hop into the sack with one of these fellows. Maybe he's tremendously built and charming. Maybe you're determined to sleep with everything in sight. After all, if Eclipse can do it, why can't you? Perhaps, you are just plain lonely and can't stand hugging your percale pillow anymore.

Yes, there are super strait-laced people who will be shocked or disgusted by this activity forecast. But be careful you don't substitute marrying the jerk to make beddy-bye legitimate. Gold rings do not a halo make. So many rushed second marriages end in divorce, that you really don't want to mistake hotpants romance for true love. If you think a first time marriage-breakup is bad for your ego, wait until your second divorce when you feel like a 200 percent total failure.

While I'm not Dr. Ruth, input from everybody tells me that first sexual encounter after your divorce is a major learning experience. You're scared, nervous, bumbling and experimental. Fortunately, no matter how brief the sexual escapade, most women report it's a darn sight better than they were getting in the marriage for the skirmish years preceding the divorce. And, if you are as naive as I was, just knowing at least one other fellow has a functional gizmo, and you don't drop dead from dealing with it, becomes a revelation unto itself.

Still, times haven't changed that much since you were a teenager. Hootchy-kootchy is not love, so when Mr. First zips up his trousers, saying he'll call you tomorrow, don't take him too literally. If you do, you may wait by the telephone, pace up and down, send him sweet little casual notes, and do anything else you can to prolong the liaison.

It's hard, when bath towels become soggy crying towels, to believe you'll ever recover, but you will. There are a lot of men out there.

Once your emotions recover from the scrambled egg syndrome, your ability to screen candidates for your affection improves a lot. Don't kick your guts around the room for having allowed yourself to be *used*. Instead, consider it your first lesson in post-marital experience. Then go optimistically on toward Lesson Two.

Some women happily report that it is possible to continue enjoying one-night stands with strangers. I don't think that's true. It's sort of like eating every meal at one of those *million-burgers-sold-today* neon-lit coops. You gulp down the sliced cardboard complete with lettuce leaf, pickle slice and synthetic dressing. But a half hour later, you can't remember what you ate, or where.

Jan tells this tale. "After my divorce, I would spend a lot of time at this cozy neighborhood bar. I would flirt and feel very popular. I would also bring a different guy home with me every night. The variety seemed just fine for a while. Then one evening I walked into the bar and saw five of my bed partners standing around talking to each other. They all waved in unison. I didn't wave back. Try as I might, I couldn't remember any of their names. Not even their first names. So I walked out, picking up my self-respect along the way."

A Modern-Day Word of Warning

I am not going to lecture in this book about STD's, the acronym for Sexually Transmitted Diseases, but do you truly want to catch something contagious and give it to every poor soul with whom you have a five-second fornication?

Such things as herpes, chlamydia, AIDS, hepatitis B, gonorrhea, and syphilis can hurt both inner and outer private parts intensely. They also can be difficult or impossible to cure. Are you immune? Do you pick your partners wisely? Do you think STD's happen only to drug users and people with alternative lifestyles?

Marianne - age 40--never married. Job: schoolteacher. Hobby: jogging.

"When I discovered I had herpes, I cried for three days. I didn't even know what it was. All of a sudden there were open sores down there. When I peed, I screamed. The pain was unbearable. I went to the doctor, and he gave me some medicine to make me feel better. He also said there was no cure and the sores would come back on and off for the rest of my life.

"The only person I could have caught it from was John, this fellow I'd been seeing. But when I met him, he told me that for business reasons he had a complete physical beforehand. He assured me he was absolutely clean.

"Afterwards, I yelled and raved at him for giving me this thing. He said he didn't know he had it. Then he disappeared. I never heard from him again. But now I'm afraid to start a relationship with anybody, because I don't want to tell them I have this disease. And I don't want to give it to them either."

Catherine - age 28--just married. Job: secretary. Hobby: shopping for clothes.

"When the doctor told me I had chlamydia, and it was passed on by sex, I said, 'Oh, I've never had sex with anybody but my husband. And we've been going together for a year.'"

So they tested her husband, and he had it. A little encounter while on a business trip. Catherine would never know about it. But now she does, and it may impair her ability to have children.

Dan - age 35--never married. Job: park ranger. Hobby: carpentry.

"I don't tell people I've got herpes. I figure it isn't catching if I'm careful and don't do anything while I have open sores. I never figured I'd get it. The woman who gave it to me looked like she was a nun."

AIDS and hepatitis B can kill you. Chlamydia and gonorrhea can have silent or easily ignored initial symptoms, so you may not discover the problem until internal damage is done. Syphilis is passed on to unborn children, resulting in terrible malformations. Herpes is transmittable with or without symptoms, and experts disagree as to whether a condom offers adequate protection.

The problem with STD's happening to "other people," is that they can pass it on to you. They may know they have a venereal disease, and not tell you. Even if you ask, point blank, they may lie. They don't want to be cut off from your love.

The smart gal is careful. Save your appetite for the gourmet experience, which shows up eventually. Celibacy is actually slightly trendy these days. The magazines and media don't push it, because sex sells copy, but the women I talk with are being very, very cautious out there on the dating scene.

First Dates and Other Fiascoes

Let's look at some examples of what you may encounter with your bewildering first dates after a divorce.

Joe was a very polite, very clean-cut young man I met during my first year of single flight. We went out for lunch, cafeteria style. On the way home, his car broke down. Since he didn't have money to pay a nearby service station, we had to push the car for about a mile through downtown traffic. Finally, we dumped the clunker near his apartment.

Joe invited me upstairs to clean up while he called his friend, the auto mechanic. Now when I say this guy was clean-cut Americana, that's an understatement. So the last thing I expected was a pass. Nor did I get one. Instead, after making his phone call, Joe disappeared into his bedroom. He re-emerged in full Nazi regalia, goose-stepping around the living room and heiling all the way.

Next adventure. A mature gentleman invited me to his home for a glass of sherry and a glimpse of a recently published volume of poems. Home base, I was told, was nearby. It wasn't. Instead, its location was in the middle of a tree-surrounded moat. Even fireflies didn't light up the total darkness.

The home's interior was no improvement. There were stuffed owls on the shelves, tables, walls, and used as bookends. Nor did the mature gentleman turn on the lights. It seems that the local electric company had disconnected the lights due to nonpayment. So we had *a* candle for light ; singular.

By the flickering illumination of this one candle, I sat and listened to poetry. I listened to every single sonnet in a rather large volume. By midnight, my complaints of migraine, dizziness, and upset stomach cleared my exit through the owl-emblazoned portal.

For a while there, I thought I would become a permanent display in the taxidermy mansion. Go ahead and snicker. After you are single a while, you'll probably be able to top that story easily.

Not all my early dates were that safe. I learned, via some mighty tight situations, never to go to a guy's apartment, home, or condominium, unless I intended to go to bed with him as soon as I entered the door. On the floor, if that was the fastest way.

I recall the incident that finally convinced me there were no safe exceptions to this rule.

Alan and I had gone to school together, way back when. Many years passed. Then, quite by chance, I met him again at a business convention. We chatted a bit, reviewed our ex-spouses, compared careers, and boasted about our respective children.

"We've got to continue this conversation over dinner sometime," Alan said. And dinner it was. By that point in my re-entry dating life, I had learned it was wiser to drive my own car and meet the new man at the site. This assured me of a sober ride home, whenever I wanted to go home. So I drove, meeting Alan at the restaurant.

The atmosphere was elegant, the wine superb, the cuisine gourmet. Conversation flowed, centered primarily on his religious experience, the importance of his good health, and the difficulty of meeting people who *respected morality.*

When the delightful dinner concluded, Alan politely invited me to his nearby ranch to see some newly purchased lambs. Being a sucker for baby anythings, I agreed.

"Come in and have a cup of coffee while you're here," Alan suggested. Why not? I found out very shortly. First Alan took my car keys and threw them across the room. Then I was reminded that his hobby was weightlifting, as he pinned me down on the couch and started working his amorous way up from my ankles. Certainly I protested. But my protestations couldn't be heard over his huffing and puffing.

In situations like this, a lady has to stay cool. Better yet, cold. I commented casually on the high cost of iceberg lettuce, the Nixon tapes, and my problems with ingrown toenails.

Unfortunately, Alan seemed to have his own built-in heating system. So I was forced, out of sheer and growing desperation, to figure out a better way to get the heck out of there.

"I've got to be home by eleven," I yelped. "My babysitter is going to quit on me."

Alan was involved in fondling the buttons on my dress. He paused for a semi-second. "How much time do I have?" he asked.

"Five minutes," I replied.

"That's okay," he said, resuming his efforts to get my million-button dress open. "I'll take what I can get."

There is nothing like a little panic to stir creative thoughts. "You know," I cooed, "I may seem reluctant, but I'm really not. After all, you're really quite an attractive man." Alan was now listening. "It's just that I have this fetish," I continued, taking heart. "It's impossible for me to enjoy sex unless I have my pale green transparent bikini nightie on."

Having gotten Alan's attention, I went on to describe how amorous, versatile and flexible this green nightie made me feel. Certainly I would be pleased to arrange a more convenient time, later in the week perhaps, when I could bring along my transparent nightie and stay "for hours."

Alan untangled himself, smoothed his muscles, and panted, "I can hardly wait," etc. Wait he did. I think after his umpteenth call, I told him I was engaged to a Sumo wrestler, or somesuch. But, like I said, I learned.

It was some years later that I expanded caution to include couples, after one indescribable episode that occurred when I was on vacation in Canada. I keep it in my mental reference, filed under "Randy and Betsy."

There are men that prey as singles, and men and women disguised as contented couples that prey on vulnerable women. When you are newly divorced you may be more vulnerable than you think. Keep in mind that some people like to swing in twos and others in threes, and if you are the conservative sort, as I am, keep your meetings with them to protected places like restaurants and conference rooms full of people. I was more shocked than harmed by Randy and Betsy's propositions, but it was unnerving. You already have enough adjusting to do.

Unless you've been single a while, you may feel I've got extraordinarily poor taste in people. Not true. The incidents above were isolated ones, but they did happen. I mention them only because, after reading of my experiences, when Mr. Yo-Yo comes your way, you won't feel like you're the only one this has ever happened to. It isn't.

Strictly for Single's Groups

There are single's groups catering to every type of person. Their activities may even be mentioned in the *About Town* section of your local or area newspaper. Single's groups can be affiliated with churches or ethnic organizations, and be geared toward tall or short people, meditation, sports, rap sessions, massage, take your pick.

Most women, after emerging from the newly-single hiding places, start with Parents Without Partners. This offers an excellent introductory umbrella and has branches in all states, plus most big and middle-size cities. It offers bridge, dances, song fests, volleyball, outings with the kids, Friday night parties, and helpful discussions on re-entry singledom.

If the branch located in Little Peach doesn't suit you, make a foray to Big Watermelon or Medium-Size Cantaloupe. As with any organization, there are groups and groups. Each one attracts its own age bracket and personality type. Do a little market research. You will eventually find the best location for your social and boyfriend shopping needs.

Of course, every time you enter a roomful of strangers, you will be frightened. The music is loud. You feel invisible. You have used up all your emotional energy just working up the nerve to leave your safe house, drive toward unknown territory, and knock on an unfamiliar door.

By the time you have placed your jacket on the pile of jackets in the back bedroom, you are ready to go home. But you don't. Instead, heart hammering in your throat, you quiver into the living room. You stand in a corner, race for the kitchen, meander toward the buffet table so you look constructively occupied. Eventually you huddle in a corner of the couch, hoping somebody comes over and rescues you.

Everybody else there seems happy, well acquainted and socially capable. As endless minutes pass, you wonder what you are doing there. You wonder when you can leave. You wonder whether you should lock yourself in the bathroom for the interim. When you try to do this, you find somebody else had the idea first.

I remember my first *go it alone,* foray. It was a local Parents Without Partners newcomer's night. I had been single for about six months, and I hadn't left the house evenings except to go to the supermarket.

Then I saw the blurb in the daily newspaper. This PWP meeting was about a mile from my house. What excuse could I give myself this time? None that sounded logical, even to my paralyzed-with-fear body.

I got into the car. Drive, drive. Little beads of sweat formed on my astringent-toned forehead. I made it to the apartment parking space. I sat in the car for eons, because my knees wouldn't move.

Finally, I got out of the car. I followed some people to the apartment door. I entered. I mumbled my name. Then I put my name tag on my coat and left my coat in the bedroom. Quickly I retreated to a chair farthest from anything, and when everybody around the room introduced themselves, I mumbled some more.

Sweat pouring down my back made my blouse stick to the upholstered chair. When the pewter tray of cheese and crackers was passed around, I took some, then couldn't chew because my mouth was too dry. I finally managed to choke down the cheese, but had to hide the crackers in the chair cushion.

For two hours, I didn't talk to anybody. I stared, sincerely, at all the others present, wondering why those perfectly decent look-ing, pleasant acting people had done something wrong and gotten divorced.

Despite it all, I must have made some type of positive impres-sion. At meeting's close, one of the perfectly pleasant gentlemen asked if he could walk me to my car.

Since walking to my car alone at night terrified me more than walking with a perfectly pleasant stranger, I accepted. By this time, my entire body had developed a severe case of terror trembles. All I wanted to do was go home, alone, and hide my head under a safe pillow.

The gentleman asked, while walking, whether I would like to go out for coffee and ice cream. At that point it wouldn't have made any difference if he was Prince Charles inviting me to a royal banquet at Balmoral Castle.

Keeping my eyes fixed on the car, I replied, without pausing, "Frankly, I don't want to go anyplace with anybody. I just want to go home and vomit. But thank you very much. Call me in a couple of weeks when maybe I will feel better. Good-bye."

I made a running dash for the car door, slammed it, turned on the ignition and peeled off into the darkness.

To my immense surprise, the gentleman did call a few weeks later, and we had a light, social evening. Eventually, I got sort of accustomed to entering a room full of single strangers. I never got totally accustomed, mind you. I don't think anybody ever feels completely at ease in this type of situation. But after the third ... or tenth ... expedition, it gets easier. At least you can swallow the cheese and get the leftover crackers as far as the wastebasket.

Be prepared to brush off the grumps or depression when you enter a solo festivity and find that most of the people are female. This happens more often than not. If you want to better the odds, Friday nights are best. Women tend to collapse with the kids after work, and men can't stand to look at an empty apartment.

However single's things are strange. You never know what will show up. For example, I went to a church function where there were four males and 144 females. My girlfriend immediately threw in the party towel and headed toward a ladies group for consolation. Meandering in the other direction, I parked myself on a corner bench next to some woebegone fellow who was overwhelmed by the hordes of females and was trying to hide.

I asked if he "felt like a sheik with a harem?" This made a good, non-threatening opener. We got into an animated conversation. One of the guy's buddies saw this, and came over from the buffet table to join us. I subsequently dated both men: a real estate agent and a taxicab owner. A rather good return for my $2.50 admission fee.

Chances are single's functions will not net you a knight in a two-piece suit, even if the male-female ratio is 10:1. So you have to find ways to keep your ego intact.

When I first started attending these groups, my sole motivation was to find a possible beau. If I didn't meet this person, or garnered more than my share of propositioning nerds, I'd go home feeling ugly, dull, insipid and moribund. In addition, I'd be super depressed.

This happened once too often, so I decided to stop laying trips on my psyche. Before I left the house, I recited the following speech to my make-up mirror: "Sweet and lovely lady. You are going out this evening to get away from the kids and the cage, to meet people, both male and female. You will have interesting conversations. You may learn something. If you don't come up with Prince Charming, at least you will have a change in scene, plus a relatively inexpensive evening. So let's knock off the pessimism and put on your best smile. At least you're trying." This speech helped my attitude immensely.

Over the years, I have pretty much stopped going to strictly-for-singles functions. Most people do stop after a while. I remember clearly the incident which prompted my exit from the solo party scene.

It was at a Halloween dance. Dressed up in my best finery, I waited on the sidelines for someone to ask me to boogie. Shortly thereafter, this sun-leathered septuagenarian parked himself next to me. He was resplendent in a shirt open to his waistline, puka-shell necklace, macho man shaving lotion, and tight white slacks.

"My name's John," he said for openers. "What's yours?"

"Pat," I replied.

"That's nice," he said. "I'm a vegetarian. Do you wanna f__?"

Shell shocked, I politely replied, "no," because I'd always been taught to be polite to my elders.

In response, John countered, "Why not? What's wrong with you?"

That evening, I went home and cried. What was wrong with me? Nothing much, I decided after a while. It was just time to move on to more constructive scenes.

Where Else to Meet Men?

The best places to meet men are work-connected activities. Don't say your job doesn't offer any prospects.

In a big company there's a community cafeteria. Go there regularly, even on your coffee breaks, and survey the scene. But keep away from going with all the ladies. Once you start with a hen group, it's hard to wriggle out. Instead, bring along a book or magazine for companionship. This not only improves you mind, but also makes a good conversation opener. I once met a nice man just because I was holding the *Wall Street Journal* at a conference lunch counter.

He said, "Anybody who reads that must be able to hold an interesting conversation."

If you work for a small company, go to the nearby luncheonette where everybody in the vicinity hangs out. It's harder to sit there alone, but not impossible. With luck, the place may get so crowded, another single will ask to join you. You may both be reading a book, but that's okay. Occasionally you both have to look up, if only to see where the ketchup is. Besides, people tend to be curious about each other. It's human nature.

Keep an ear open for conventions or seminars which have any relation to the job you're doing. You can stretch that quite a bit. For example, while going through divorce proceedings, I was sitting in my attorney's office leafing through a magazine. There was a notice about a lawyer's meeting dealing with new changes in the divorce laws. The notice didn't say the meeting was limited to lawyers. I figured I might learn something, and sent in the nominal fee.

I certainly did learn something, it was quite an update on my legal rights. Not so much the lectures, but the shop talk around them. I also met a very interesting attorney who happened to be sitting next to me in the conference room.

Opportunities for constructive socializing present themselves every place you turn, if you keep your eyes—and mind—open. No matter what position you have, and this includes being the basement janitor, you've got multiple facets attached to that position.

For example, as a janitor you work with a multitude of cleaning products. Some manufacturers give free how-to seminars. If in doubt, write and ask, "I am maintenance supervisor at Lady's Church School and am very pleased with your product. I would like to learn more about it and your company. Are there any seminars scheduled in my area, Europe, China, Big Apple?"

If nothing else, you'll get an appreciative letter in reply. With luck, you'll get a lead on how to proceed further. When I was involved in hospital work, I attended physician seminars and administrative seminars. My job only fringed on these professions. But it fringed enough to be employment related, and therefore tax deductible. I met some interesting people. In addition, my supervisors were impressed by my ambition and tidbits of added knowledge, leading to a couple of pay increases.

Whatever job I'm doing, I keep my ears open for any dinner or business meetings which might help me do that job better. These meetings also give me leads on job opportunities.

In the course of moving and improving yourself, you will meet men who think as you do. They will respect you for what you've become. They will also admire you for being sane and stable while single, this being a rarity. Men have just as difficult a time meeting healthy women as you have problems meeting healthy men.

Should work related groups turn you off, there are other special interest groups to consider. These include: wine tasting, bridge, model railroads, coins, stamps, guns, antique cars, motorcycles, trivia, and chess. Don't be afraid someone will turn down your membership fee because you don't know diddlydots about the subject. I've only been turned down once, and that was for a forensic pathology group.

In most instances, the presumption is you're willing to learn, and have an interest in the topic. All groups like new members. That's what keeps them going. So scout around, attend a meeting or two, and see what suits your fancy.

Still not plugged in? Then go back to school for an accounting, furniture construction, or auto mechanic basic course. I once met a very likable fellow in a sign language course.

There are also short sessions, advertised in your local newspaper, dealing with investing, real estate, and how to save money on taxes. If you listen carefully, and don't invest in any oil wells in the middle of a Florida game preserve, you will surely learn something valuable about money. You may not have any now, but you do hope to earn some.

Many men have confided to me that they have trouble meeting women who aren't "dingbats," "looking for a meal ticket," or "on some way-out mental tangent." These men go to the same classes, meetings, and seminars that you will be attending. Although they may deny it, quite a few go for reasons which have little to do with the lecture topic. Still, the topic gives everybody a conversational gambit, which beats what-do-we-talk-about? single's functions every time. Given the brave new world you have entered, it takes a bit of nerve, to make it a world you will truly enjoy.

Bring a Girlfriend for Company

If you don't like to venture out alone, try to find a female friend to accompany you. Whenever possible, pick someone of similar intellect and thinking. If you don't, you will have a dead weight on your hands.

All too many times I've talked an acquaintance into joining me for a learning activity. Halfway through the lecture, she is ready to leave. Stay for the social function? Never. You end up with a compromise that pleases no one. So discuss it beforehand and agree on your adventure rules.

First, agree to split up on entering the social or learning event. Do not clump together like soapsuds. Splitting up makes it a lot easier for one guy who wants to talk to one of you, but doesn't have the nerve to approach a battalion.

Second, discuss your departure time, and fix it firmly beforehand. If you don't, toward mid-evening one of you may be surrounded by multiple Robert Redfords, while the other has been talking to a potted plant for an hour and wants to go home. If the bored person is driving, lively lady has a problem. The same is true when the situations are reversed. A nice, firm commitment to leave at 11:00 p.m. really does work best.

Third, you must make a commitment to leave together. I remember going to a dance with a female friend who, someplace during the course of the evening, decided to take off without letting me know. It was no fun looking through coat closets and ladies bathrooms for Ms. Inconsiderate Houdini. I kept thinking she was crumpled in a corner with her throat cut. After several hours, I found out she had gathered her coat and gone home.

Leaving together is also a protective device. Otherwise you might be tempted to go joy riding with some jerk you just met, and it might not turn out to be such a joy ride after all. A girlfriend's presence eliminates the need to end the festivities with a bout of kung-fu.

There are instances where you, or your girlfriend, will meet a charming person who wants to go out for a midnight snack. When this happens, you should both go, in your car, not his, and meet at the restaurant. If you can, try to convince Mr. Charming to bring along a buddy. Otherwise, two females tend to get into conversational competition, and shortly thereafter want to start a hairpulling contest.

Who picks up the tab? I figure if a guy can't afford to pick up the check for coffee and donuts for two gals on a diet, he can't afford anything, so you don't need him, anyway. My girlfriend tells me to get modern, women pick up their own checks. She says it makes you more independent. This is something you have to work out for yourself, because you know your comfort zone.

Will all these tiny rules discourage a prospective suitor? A man who is interested *is interested.* If you have to leave at 11:00 p.m. with your girlfriend, and he wants your phone number, he will ask for it. If you think he needs a little push, say, "I'm sorry I have to leave, but I hope to see you again." Should that not have the desired effect, the dude's either a dunce, too terrified to be of much use at this point, or not intrigued. Better hunting next round.

Sauntering Forth Solo

You may eventually choose to attend single's functions or other activities alone. Often you can't find anyone to go with you. Sometimes you get tired of being accompanied by a ball and chain.

If you decide to go alone, particularly at night, make double certain you get excellent driving instructions. Ask about parking availability, too. Wending your way through remote wheat fields, walking three blocks on a deserted street, or wandering your way through dark condominium pathways is nerve wracking as well as dangerous.

When you venture forth alone, set a mental departure hour. I tell myself, "If I don't meet someone interesting by 11:00 p.m., I'll go home without loss of face." Hanging around until doomsday in hopes of scoring big leads to massive dejection. This doesn't help your ego the next time you want to get out of the house, and you have to go someplace by yourself.

In summation, it's not the wisest course of action to leave your car on the street and enter a stranger's automobile. I don't care how adorable he is. Give him your phone number. Let him call. Meet him at a time and place where you can let your kids and your babysitter know the location and your gentleman friend's name. I know this may sound like old-fashioned nagging, but you would truly like to grow old gradually—not overnight. If you go to a single's function by yourself and meet someone interesting who wants to go out afterward, get in your own car and meet him at a well-lit restaurant.

Depending on whether you swing, rock, or wobble, at least once you may find yourself at a solo function that doesn't mesh with your moral standards. For example, I was invited to an afternoon swim party by a work acquaintance. It was a big surprise to find myself the only one there who expected to wear a bathing suit.

As soon as you see trouble brewing, get out! In this situation, most of the party crew was getting fairly drunk. I was in danger of being pushed in the pool, at the least. Polite, as always, I picked up my bag and towel, and excused myself to visit the bathroom. From this sanctuary, I made my way quietly out the back door, where I met a fellow also sneaking out.

We had a very nice chat someplace else. Although we weren't each other's types, we both had a nice quiet afternoon. In this instance, my going to the party alone had definite advantages. The girlfriend I had thought of inviting as company was into nudity. I would have spent the whole swimming pool session locked in the loo—out of embarrassment!

You will encounter, until you learn more about the various single's groups, those that are into pot, alcohol, and coke. You will also encounter rap sessions that can turn into rather vicious analysis.

Walk out the same way you came in, or any other way. Do it five minutes after you enter. If the scene is not for you, nobody there will be for you. You'll accomplish more going home and cleaning the oven.

While some rap sessions are negative, others can be quite beneficial. Ask around. Kaiser Health Plan offers self-help groups, Second Chance does, Alcoholics Anonymous does, etc. As a note, if you were married to an alcoholic, I strongly recommend going to at least a few sessions of Al-Anon. This group is for the family of alcoholics, and you will learn a tremendous amount about yourself. If you don't understand co-dependency, your next mate may have the same problem.

While some women have met nice beaus at self-help groups, I always figured I had enough problems without picking up on any-body else's. One gal who married a millionaire she met at AA, disagrees. She went, and she never touches a drop. "Good place to go husband hunting," she said.

The bar scene is not for me, but many of my women friends enjoy the bustle and camaradie of a friendly neighborhood bar. There are also the bars at major hotels, which have a little more pizzazz.

The problem with bars is the number of married men there who are on holiday from their wives. You can sit on a bar stool all evening long and hear many slurred propositions. You will get knee gropies. Your telephone number will be requested. It may even be used.

You also run a risk of being mugged on your way back through the bar or hotel parking lot to the car. The later you emerge from the bar, the higher the risk, because the drunker everybody is. While I've met women who have met winners over double scotch-on-the-rocks, most bar habitués meet rockheaded losers.

However, if you tend to imbibe freely, desperately need company, and don't mind paying good money for 90 percent water, then visit a high-class bar and socialize. I tend to be hopelessly old fashioned.

You may find a bar where it is possible to meet sober single persons, who make a good living, don't practice feelies, and have a deep respect for pickups. A possibility, like I said.

Blind Dates: Delight or Disaster

"Blind date!" my girlfriend exclaims. "I would never go out on a blind date." Sandi, over the years, has gone door to door peddling chocolate bars, magazine subscriptions, and you-too-can-be-beautiful cosmetics. She has sat, for seeming ages, in tacky living rooms and rancid kitchens, helping some stranger decide between *Better Burp and Gargle* and *Good Floorsweeping* magazines. But go out for a jelly donut with somebody she's never met? Heaven forbid!

Why the donut shop might be a *seraglio* (a harem-like depository of fresh females) for Jack the Ripper and the blind date a stand-in for Vulpi the Werewolf. "A person would have to be very desperate to agree to a situation like that," Sandi says with a shudder. If you agree, you're not alone, so do a lot of other people.

The term "blind date" has three generally accepted definitions. (1) You would have to be blind not to die of fright upon looking at the other person. (2) The other person would have to be blind not to die of fright upon meeting you. (3) For the upcoming meeting, it is better that both of you are deaf, too.

This attitude isn't limited to women. Men are also skittish about blind dates. For example, Steve sells real estate. He would probably climb Mt. Kilimanjaro in mid-winter to meet Medusa, if he thought she would invest in a piece of nearby income property.

Steve is a bachelor. I asked him if he'd like to meet my very delightful second cousin, who had recently arrived in the community. I might as well have offered him cyanide. "A person would have to be pretty desperate to think about something like that," he said.

Both Sandi and Steve has said many times how difficult it is to meet interesting, sane, single people about their own age. Does this tune sound familiar? So why is there such a problem when some sympathetic soul tries to run interference?

Let's look at the situation from another angle. It's a very quiet Friday night and you want a change in pace. You pass up the newspaper or single's group list of activities. A single's party best meets your mood.

You get all dressed up and go to the party. Festivities are in full decibel. You look for someone whose face and/or personality seems attractive. Unfortunately, that one person is surrounded by fifteen admirers and you can't get through the mob.

You retreat to the chip and dip table. A fellow muncher is standing there, also. You exchange glances. "Not my type," is the mutual thought.

Soon you return to the party, clutching your celery stalks. Mr. Attractive has disappeared. Everybody else looks dull, inebriated, or engaged. You wish you were home. Soon you are. "Where are all the available guys?" you mutter for weeks afterward.

Mr. Attractive was available, but if someone offered to fix you up with him, sight unseen, you probably would have turned the offer down. The fellow at the chip and dip table was available, too. If you had actually talked to him for a bit, you would have found him quite congenial. But your self-selection processes stop you from discovering how much you have in common. These are the same self-selection processes that you used to find your ex-husband. Maybe somebody could do a better job for you?

At an arranged meeting, a term I prefer to *blind date,* you could have talked with the quieter fellow. Perhaps you would have made a friend, perhaps a lover. How much risk is there, if the twosome is connived by someone who knows you both? I've met quite a few interesting men through mutual friends. I wouldn't have met these gentlemen otherwise, given luck and a certain inate reclusiveness.

I've also introduced several people, often spending quite a bit of time persuading them to take a chance. Some of these introductions have turned out quite well. A few have resulted in marital bliss, although that wasn't my original intention. I just wanted two nice people to meet each other in this big wide world.

What about Vulpi the Werewolf or Jack the Ripper's seraglio? If you follow a few basic rules, nobody runs into many problems: (1) The matchmaker must know both of you well enough to almost guarantee mutual attraction through jelly donuts and coffee. (2) A snack it is, so neither party has to worry about picking up the few-buck tab. (3) The meeting should take place at a not-too-crowded restaurant. It should not take place in the woods, apartment of either party, or any other isolated nook or cranny. (4) Conversation should be kept casual. If either party starts talking about sex, ideas germinate like weeds. Discuss ice hockey, the stock market, or how to cook chili. (5) Don't go expecting Adonis, Hercules, or Woody Allen. Disappointment shows in both facial expression and mannerisms. Give the other person the same courtesy you expect. He may turn out to be fascinating, despite the lack of a cleft chin and bulging biceps.

Sometimes blind dates lead to further meetings, sometimes they don't. My experience has been that like, or not like, is usually mutual. If the person doesn't excite you, at least you've spent an hour or so in new conversation. This beats watching television reruns.

If the person is super, then a genie has taken part in your dating future. What you thought of as a possible disaster has turned out to be a genuine delight.

Sometimes You Get a Fig

You will meet an intriguing variety of men now that you are again single. Some of them weren't highly visible when you were younger.

He lives with Mother. It constantly amazes me how many grown men still reside with their mothers. Their stories are rather consistent. "I tried living on my own, but frankly it was very expensive. Mom (who is usually a widow or long-time divorcee) has this big house. It seems silly for us both to be making house (or rent) payments. Of course Mom has her life and I have mine. In fact, I seldom see her. She's usually in bed by the time I come home. Even if awake, she's in her room watching television. So it's really like having the house all to myself. I come and go as I please."

If you meet Mom, you will find her a very pleasant person, quite polite and hospitable. She is also extremely determined that Junior will live with her as long as they both shall live. As a note, she will probably outlive you and Junior, too. Not that she doesn't encourage Junior to marry *someday.* She does, at least verbally. But she also answers the phone for him, cooks 14-course meals, washes his clothes, irons his undies, and makes his bed. In one instance I know of, Mom also washes Junior's feet when he comes home from a hard day on the road.

Junior has the motivation to marry like he has the motivation to jump off a bridge. Should he ever get even the slightest urge toward wedding bells, Mom's techniques make guerrilla warfare seem subtle. She talks of the terror of her own marriage, tells ample scare stories of predatory cat women, offers dire predictions of venereal disease. In addition there's "I'm sick. I'm feeble. I only have a few more painful years left." All this works well on certain male types, and very well indeed on Junior.

He's been married at least twice. In these days of sequential matrimony, you will meet many men who have been married before, and before that. They are often quite charming. As a whole, they like to socialize.

It does not always come out that Hubert was married before, but you may eventually hear dire tales of what his wife (singular) was like. And, in the course of your relationship, slips of tongue occur that are not particularly romantic.

He refers to Hannah instead of Heloise, for example. Or to children you've never heard of. So you ask. Hubert's reply sounds like this, "Oh, yes. That. I was just a kid (i.e., someplace between 17 and 27). The marriage didn't last very long (translation: only five years and a couple of kids long)."

This really doesn't mean much, for anybody can make a mistake—or two, or three. But you should realize that men who have been married twice before can be extremely reluctant to take the plunge again. Or even to get truly committed again.

If your multimarried new beau is the opposite type, wanting to get married again immediately, you should exercise some caution here, too. It pays you to do some sleuthing, a practice many modern women are paying detectives for, and find the cost well worth it. Sleuthing is especially valuable if you have a few bucks to your name and wish to protect your bank account.

A friend, call her "Gullible," chose not to try a detective investigation when she met the man of her dreams. He was retired military, complete with pension. He was courteous, seemed to adore her children, and apparently had ample income.

Mr. Dreams did mention, in passing, that he hadn't spoken to his own children since his divorce. This is a definite warning sign, but Gullible chose to ignore it. It also came out that Mr. Dreams had a few *liaisons* since his marriage failed, one of which happened to be another marriage. "But it was so brief," he explained hastily, "I could barely call it that."

Gullible didn't press the issue. She thought Mr. Dreams was such a gentleman, only a fool wouldn't appreciate him. And he did so want to get married, and so did she. So they did get married. It lasted exactly three weeks. Mr. Dreams became very upset when Gullible refused to transfer all her monies to his name. "After all, I'm the man of the house now," he said.

Mr. Dreams, it turned out, really didn't like children at all. Children cost quite a bit to feed and clothe. It also came out that Mr. Dreams had been married at least three times. His wives were so glad to get rid of him that they gave him cash settlements.

When Gullible, getting smarter rapidly, started checking on his *pension,* it turned out to be for psychiatric disability. This was manifested during her brief non-bliss when Mr. Dreams shot two of the neighbors' cats because they were making too much noise.

The marriage was very traumatic for Gullible and very profitable for the lawyer she employed to get her out of it. Even the briefest of checks beforehand would have shown enough blips to make her think twice about the arrangment.

When a man who's been married several times wants to marry again immediately, it doesn't hurt to ask a few pertinent questions. Follow up the answers with some research. It's not that you don't trust or love the apparent gentleman, but business is business. While being single has its ups and down, a rotten second marriage only has its downs.

Men who like men. You are not going to change him, so if you choose to get involved with a man who prefers male partners, be prepared for a lot of competition from males. You do not have the equipment to cope with this. To survive you will have to be extraordinarily openminded. You will also spend a lot of time by yourself, or with your beloved's boyfriends.

Most sane women have the smarts to stay away from this situation. But it is also possible to become involved with a homosexual male without realizing what you are doing. Maureen's example is a typical one.

Brought up in a good Christian home, she became disgusted with the clutch and grab routine which is part of the modern dating scene. When she met Stuart, she was delighted to find someone who knew how to treat a lady like a lady.

In their six month courtship, Stuart would put his arm around her, and enjoyed necking in the car. He never attempted to go much further than that. "I have too much respect for you," he explained. "The rest comes with marriage." Could a lady find a better catch?

Stuart was an attractive, rugged looking man, he earned a steady living, and he was honest, thoughtful and kind. He also adored Maureen's two children. Still, a sardine would have been a better marital catch. Stuart was motivated to marry her by his need to cover an involvement with a male supervisor, which was subtly endangering his promotional opportunities in a rather conservative firm.

Unlike Mr. Dreams, Stuart actually intended to be a good husband. He had only one drawback, and Maureen found out about that when their post-matrimonial sex life dwindled from mediocre to nothing rather rapidly. It wasn't quite what the lady had bargained for, and it took several years of weeping, self-accusation and counseling to rid herself of the pain.

While the chances of this happening to you are slim, they are not unheard of. It can be extremely difficult to weed out the male who prefers males from the male who actually respects you enough to keep his paws off the merchandise. Try to meet his friends, not just his co-workers. Make it a point to join your beau at office functions, then listen to the scuttlebut. And remember not to let your new love sweep you right off your feet and into a second marriage.

Men who like lots of women. Casanovas have their own special motivations. "If I date just one gal," says one gent, "there's a chance I'll get involved. But when I date several, of course they don't know about each other, I'm protected from getting too deeply into any relationship."

David describes his system this way. "I see Sue on Monday night. Jan on Tuesday night. Carol on Friday night. Beth visits Saturday." On Sunday he rests.

None of his girlfriends are allowed to just drop in. Should one show up at his apartment door, she is not allowed to enter because David is on his way out, terribly busy, or sick in bed with something contagious. His manner discourages entry while being polite. "I'd love to chat with you, my darling, but not at this moment. Why didn't you call first?"

After a while, Sue, Jan, Carol, and Beth get properly trained and stick to their alloted night. They also learn not to make phone calls to David, other than 30-second ones, because he always has something burning on the stove, or he is on his way out the door, or he is in the midst of fixing some gizmo that just can't wait.

This type of man may seem convenient to those with busy schedules or into the same type of revolving door concept, but it's a real ego dampener to realize why you are forever consigned to Tuesday. It's also dangerous, given all those STD's that could be making the rounds from Saturday gal—to David—to yours truly.

If you want a beau that's always busy, find one who is really wrapped up in his work. That is probably why his wife left, but it may also be your preference.

Men who are secretly married. You are inevitably going to meet men, in the course of business, social outings, or single's parties who keep their marital state a total secret.

Some women actually gravitate deliberately toward married men. "They take you to such lovely places, buy expensive gifts, and are so romantic," goes the refrain. But let's presume you are not into the kind of masochism these gals set themselves up for, and wish to make certain Mr. Splendid is single. You also wish to know this quickly, since waiting until your three-month dating anniversary, when you are madly in love and wildly entangled, makes it a lot more difficult to get uninvolved.

To find out whether a man is truly single, listen to his conversation carefully. Married men will often slip, using the pronoun "we" instead of "I," or "our" instead of "my." For example, "We decided to buy a new car," "We always jog in the mornings," etc., or "our dog," "our second home," "our collection of antique horseshoes." Married men who run around often have extensive practice in avoiding such giveaway words. However, eventually, if he talks long enough, and if this is accompanied by a cocktail, these telltale words usually show up.

When you hear "we," casually ask who *we* is. Mr. Splendid will mumble, stutter, come up with some vague but possibly adequate response suggesting his mother, daughter, fourteen kids, prior girlfriend, live-in girlfriend who is leaving that very afternoon, or whatever. Don't take that at face value. Stay alert.

Where and how does Mr. Splendid spend his weekends and vacations? This is an innocent question to ask, since you do truly want to find out what you have in common. Should his response be something like, "I stay home and fix up the house," run up a little white flag. Single men may spend some hours puttering, but usually prefer emphasizing walking on the beach, ski trips, or long soulful drives in the countryside.

However, you still aren't certain of his status, so look fascinated and ask about his children. After all, you like to mention your own children from time to time. Mr. Splendid is also entitled to that privilege. Since this query seems harmless enough, chances are he'll answer honestly, albeit perhaps briefly, with their ages and gender. Your immediate follow-up question is, "Do they live with you?"

Since he will most probably tell you they live with their mother, you now have an opening to ask where she lives. If he starts being vague, or takes evasive verbal action, set off alarm bells. It's quite easy to say Cecily lives in Chicago, West Point, or three blocks away. The response is automatic, if there's no reason to fib.

There is a quicker method. When he asks you out, get his home phone number in case something unexpected comes up. If he gives you his work number, again request his home number. I don't care if he's a surgeon on 24-hour radio page. If no home number is forthcoming, consider the guy married.

Is it always necessary to be sneaky? Can't you just ask upfront "Are you married?" You can, and I just about always do so these days, perhaps couching it sweetly with, "Surely a good-looking man like you must be married?" This isn't rude, it's just practical. Single men may actually respect you for asking. Many single men don't like women who willingly date married men. So if you ask, that's okay. Nobody single will be offended.

There are times when you should tiptoe around the topic. Single life is full of complexities. Suppose you meet a very nice fellow at a business conference. He is extra attentive, helpful, and chock full of valuable information. He may even invite you to the local luncheonette to further exchange information.

This man is actually being friendly, in the same way a new woman acquaintance might be friendly. If you come right out and ask if he's married, right in the middle of your ham sandwich or a discussion of computer programming, you are implying motives which may not be there. This nice guy will take off like a bat out of Hades, hoping you are not chasing behind.

Too blunt a procedure can cut you off from a valuable business contact. And if the nice guy knows people you know, you can get an undeserved locker room reputation. Men gossip more than women about some things.

Safe and Sane Review

Do not invite a man you have just met to your home, apartment or hotel room unless you are prepared to sleep with him, willingly or unwillingly. I don't care how feeble the guy looks, how innocent, or how charming. Men think differently than women about such invitations. You might be issuing an invitation to a wrestling party.

When going on a date with a man you are not quite sure you want to get involved with, go for lunch. Mention an appointment in two hours, putting a time limit on the occasion. Daylight keeps conversation bright and shiny. When you exit, you have a few days to think about whether you want to encourage the friendship or not. If the fellow interests you, chances are you will interest him. If he doesn't jibe with your hormones, it's easier to get out of it during a phone call than at the close of dinner complete with champagne.

If you opt for the wining and dining scene with a relative stranger, go to a nice public place. Should your date demonstrate such quirks as heavy drinking or talking about sexy leather straps, don't bother to be polite. Excuse yourself to the powder room and don't bother to return.

On a first date, or even a second, drive your own car. Should you want to offer a reason for this, use convenience. Tell him you don't want to make him come a distance to pick you up, therefore you will meet him wherever. If the date doesn't turn out nicely, it's a relief to drive yourself home.

Sometimes a fellow you think is pleasant invites you to his place for dessert and expresso. Beware! While the majority of males are lovely humans, a few can be a real pain. It takes a lot of talking to get yourself out of jeopardy safely, if you can.

All the above advice will become second nature to you after you have been single a while. You develop a sort of radar system that warns of impending bombers and bombs. However, the first few years of re-entry dating tend to be filled with mental and physical pitfalls. Some assaults leave new scars on your already bruised psyche, while others just leave you shell-shocked. If you learn how to duck when the warning sirens whistle, re-entry is just a little bit easier.

Will You Meet Someone Wonderful?

The most wonderful person you will meet during your quest is you. You will do this by expanding activities, getting acquainted with new people, and gaining control over your life. Should a wonderful world include, to your mind, a new and gentler spouse, this is also a definite possibility. Where he will turn up is anybody's guess.

Diane met her husband while standing in line at a bank. Marilyn met Ben at a community college self-hypnosis class. Carla changed churches after her divorce and married the new minister, who was a widower. Karen did a fender bender in a supermarket parking lot and got insurance money—and the guy.

I also have several friends who found wedded bliss via single's functions. Their stories go something like: "Well, I didn't feel like going anyplace that night, least of all to a wine and cheese party where I would just stand around in a corner, as usual. But I promised to bring a tray of crackers/my guitar/my record player. So I decided to make a brief appearance and leave as soon as possible. But this guy, whom I had never seen before, kept following me around. So the party actually turned out quite well after all."

None of these women reported fantastic sparks at the first encounter. The men were not heroes from romantic novels. A few were tall and lanky. Sometimes the gals opted to wear low heels in order not to tower over their new beau; the intellectual found the non-intellectual a welcome relief from the brainstorming that went on at work; the trendy dresser discovered she preferred someone who admired her, rather than competed with her. All had learned from their prior marriage that a real person is not a series of statistics: height, weight, biceps, sexual endurance, IQ, or bank balance. The women also had something else in common; most were extremely hesitant to enter another marriage.

"But Joe kind of grew on me," Carla says with a contented smile. "Where my former husband thought housework was beneath him, Joe pitches in and does the dishes without being asked. Before, when I was ill or out of sorts, my ex-husband would find an excuse to work late. Joe sets aside whatever he is doing and takes the time to listen. He makes me a cup of tea, massages my forehead.

"There are no diamond birthday gifts in this marriage," Carla continues. "With two sets of kids to support, we can't afford that. But there are always flowers, a thoughtful gift, a personally selected card. And they're all given on time."

Joe is trying harder this round. So is Carla. So will you.

Finding Mr. Truly Wonderful will take a while—don't rush it. There's a lot to learn about yourself. There's a lot of nonsense to clear out of your brain. You want a relationship that will grow. One that allows space. One that will last. That relationship may be just around the corner, a mile down the road, or 10 miles up the mountain. But it comes along, usually when you least expect it. In the meantime, there's a new world to explore. Part of that new world is discovering who you are.

THE PATTER
OF LITTLE FEET

So you try sneaking *him* in. After all, it's after 2:00 a.m., and the kids are sound asleep. Where are you expected to have a romantic encounter, in the garage?

You are careful. You tiptoe. You drape a bathrobe over the bedroom doorknob, nobody should be able to peek through the keyhole.

"Be careful how you get on the bed," you whisper. "It has a creaky spot in the lower left hand corner, about where Mickey Mouse is chasing Pluto."

He avoids the creaks. You pull the discounted Disneyland sheets up to your necks and amour takes over. More or less.

If your kids are within 400 miles, your amour tends to go like this: "Stop saying anything, even if it's nice," "Can you moan and groan more quietly," and "Stop leaping up and down like that, you're making the bedsprings creak."

Right when the going gets good, and the good gets going, you say, "Stop for a minute." You think you hear one of the kids. "No. It's just the cat. Okay. But can you hurry it up?" You are getting nervous.

Lady Chatterly probably enjoyed sex more with her husband than you did that evening. But the evening wasn't over yet. Sleep, for youngsters, is a rare phenomenon—like Halley's Comet.

At your worried suggestion, Romeo hurriedly puts on his red jockey shorts and street clothes and is pushed out the door. Exactly 3 minutes later, in rushes Junior. He smashes through the feeble lock on your bedroom door, dashing blindly to your bed in total darkness. Then, with a desperate gurgle, he upchucks four slices of pizza with anchovies, two squares of garlic bread, and a fudge sundae complete with maraschino cherry.

This wonderful concoction splats all over the portion of mattress covered by Mickey Mouse chasing Pluto. After you recuperate, which takes a few years, recalling the scene makes you chuckle. If Romeo had remained just a little while longer, the kid's upchuck would have landed right on his ....

Anyhow, from then on, you go over to Romeo's house. Your children get some logical excuse for your absence, like Mommy wants to play checkers/chess/computer games in peace and quiet.

But it's never quite that easy. These are modern times, and Romeo may have kids at his house, either because he's the permanent custodial parent or he has weekend visitation. If his bedroom walls are as thin as yours, you still hush and shush each other all evening long. Then you get to drive home, dark, cold, and alone, hoping your clunker-car doesn't collapse on the freeway.

Anybody who envies the swinging, fantastic sex life of the single parent has got glue in lieu of imagination. You are trying to raise children as decent, moral, scholarly, non-pregnant human beings. In order to do this, you must set a good example. Translation: You may be able to have a love life, but Junior doesn't have to know all—or anything—about it.

Youngsters love to chat as much as adults. Junior will chat about your activities to friends, who will tell their parents, who will tell all the people they know. Junior may also get upset at this stranger latching onto his mother's heart, or body, and start doing really poor work at school. And your own budding Juliet may eventually use your example as an excuse for bringing her own Mr. Wonderful onto your living room couch.

No matter how much you protest, your common sense tells you it's "monkey see, monkey do." Like most conscientious parents, you have dreams of the next generation living the good life.

Even if you display the purity of a sterilized surgical glove, you may still have a wayward kid or two. But at least you won't hear, "You're a fine one to lecture," along with a recital of past sins you'd just as soon consign to oblivion. Virtue has some solace.

They're Too Young to Understand

I used to believe my children were too young to understand. Don't bet on it. One day I overheard a conversation between my 7-year-old and a friend.

They'd gone to a slumber party. They talked about it for weeks afterward. The evening had been spent, not slumbering, but listening. About 3 a.m. the party girl's parents, thinking they were surely safe, had enjoyed some connubial exercises. The party guests, at their hostess's invitation, had gotten water glasses and pressed them against the wall. Each romantic sound was quite amplified and appreciated. The kids described everything, in detail.

In today's world, where television and movies are disgustingly graphic, and pop songs give play by play accounts of body work, children "too young" to understand, hear more than they should. They understand plenty of it, too, much more than you ever did at their age.

The only thing you can do is acknowledge this comprehension. Nobody says you have to like it. This means you don't shove your love life under a child's nose. Kids desperately want to believe that Mommy is not one of *those,* and truly would like to pretend she's a virgin altogether. They will do this, given any excuse whatsoever. All you have to do is practice discretion.

Introducing Whassis Name

The procession of males meandering through and around your castle, at sporadic intervals or in glops, will lead to some itchy situations with the kids. It's best if you learn how to scratch effectively.

For example, you met the guy at a noisy dance. While you can remember his name is Rodney, you aren't sure whether his surname is White, Wicki, or Whizinkinski. Nor do you know much more about him, except that he seems to be some type of plumbing salesman ... or is it plumber? ... or does he make plumb bobs?

Rodney doesn't slouch, has a cute mustache, and smiles nicely. So you have graciously given him your phone number. He uses it a few weeks later, being faced with the prospect of a dateless weekend. Presto, you have a movie invitation.

You primp and pretty beforehand, light a household fumigation candle, and remove all skateboards from the driveway. This activity draws immediate attention from the junior set. "What are you doing?" Junior asks. This is followed by "Why?" and "Who for?"

Constant interrogation makes you apply your eyelash curler to your eyeball, but Junior doesn't let up. Telling Junior to go away gets no results; children won't go. Eventually you say "I'm going out to a movie with Rodney."

"Rodney, who?"

"Rodney, duh ..."

"Where did he come from?"

"He *came* from a dance I went to."

"Is he like the last one you brought home?"

"No, this one uses a deodorant."

"Where is he taking you?"

"I told you. To a movie."

"Which one?"

"*The Rise and Fall of Humidifiers.*"

"That's rotten. Besides, it's rated 'R.'"

"Mind your own business."

"What time are you coming home?"

"I don't know."

"Are you going to let him kiss you?"

"Go watch television."

"Why should I? Talking to you is more interesting."

It's little wonder, when the doorbell rings, you grab coat and cap, and make a mad dash for the exit. Rodney gets a quick glimpse of your motley brood, who are all lined up and staring at his Adam's apple.

Quickly, before he figures out the place is a madhouse, he is not-too-gently shuffled out. But you don't escape unscathed. The youngest offspring bellows out, "What time are you coming home?" Since you don't have an immediate answer, you say "duh."

That *duh* sound is the closest thing to saying dumb. However, it took me much longer than it should have to figure it out. I finally caught on one evening when returning from a blind date. The kids were all awake at midnight, one of them near tears. The poor babysitter was beside herself.

"They kept telling me you went out with someone you didn't even know," she said. Then she added, "They were afraid you were going to leave them, just like their father did."

After that, I developed a fairly set format. I get my date's moniker by hook or by crook. The easiest way is to ask Rodney what his last name is. If this makes you feel like a dork for accepting a date with someone who has no last name, then ask Rodney to spell his last name. This gives you a reputation for accuracy. He may spell "Jones" or "Smith." But that could be "Jownes" or "Smyth," one never knows.

Prior to Rodney's arrival, I pass on to the children whatever information I have. If I don't have any information, then I tell an anecdote or two, something to make Rodney's appearance less threatening. For example, "I met Rodney at a dance that I went to with second cousin Edith. He was the only fellow there with a plaid suede jacket. Well, you know what crazy taste I have in clothes. And it was such a smashing jacket, sort of orange and green. He started telling me about some type of plumbing work that he does. It was very interesting. So we're going out to a movie to talk some more."

When Rodney arrives, he is ushered into the kitchen. He is then introduced to all the children, and possibly offered a cup of coffee. In the time it takes to drink a cup of coffee, all the kids can inspect him to their heart's content. Only then do we leave.

I tell the babysitter and the children where we are going to be. If the evening is sort of hit and miss, I promise to call home in an hour and give my location. I do this promptly. I also state what time I'm going to return home.

Never arrive home late. It is best to arrive home a smidge early. This is very important, especially the first year after a divorce. Younger children, and the older ones too, are truly quite terrified that Mommy will desert them, vanish into thin air, or be harmed. This will leave them with no parents at all. Valid or not, this is how they feel.

Your verbal assurances will not solve this problem. You need to be absolutely reliable! After a while their panic will cease, although it always seems to be an undercurrent in a single parent household. Your major respite is when the children get to be dating teenagers, and begin coming home later than you do. But that's another worry, for another time.

Rodney Becomes a Regular

You are somewhat smitten with virile, handsome and/or brainy Rodney. The feeling is apparently reciprocated. So the gentleman becomes a regular at your doorstoop. His name becomes well known to the family. Younger children react to this new aspect of their lives with an unending set of giggles.

"It's you know who on the phone again, Mommy," giggle, giggle, smirk, twitter. If you have a phone extension, they will make every attempt to listen to your conversation.

You usually hear their heavy breathing, and eventually shout "Get off the phone, you nerd." If your voice is loud enough to frighten the kiddy eavesdropper, it is also loud enough to rupture Rodney's eardrums. Since you want him to think you are truly forever sweet-voiced, you now have to make feeble excuses. Otherwise he will think you are not quite the wonderful woman he thought you were a moment ago.

There is only one way to avoid this dilemma. When Wee Curiosity gets on the phone extension, and your coos of "Please hang up, darling. This is a private call," do not get results, excuse yourself to answer the doorbell. Run rapidly into the other room. Pop Junior's posterior slightly, or utter massive threats with a fierce expression. This should earn you about 10 minutes peace and quiet.

After 10 minutes, one of Junior's siblings will start listening in. You then have to repeat the threats. There's no way of actually winning this little game, but at least you save Rodney's hearing. You also get to preserve the image you wish to preserve.

As the relationship continues apace, so do the questions dreamed up by your little sugarplums. For example, one evening my then-5-year-old daughter watched me get dressed for a date. "Mommy," she asked, a puzzled expression on her cherubic face, "why are you wearing your good underpants with the lace? Nobody's going to see them, are they?"

Since you are trying to preserve the impression that late evening hours will be spent in a nunnery, you get to be imaginative about how everybody should always look their best at all times, from inside out, regardless of whether anybody sees them or not.

This type of malarky suffices for a while. Remember, children of all ages really *want* to believe. Unfortunately, when the youngsters get to the age of knowing that birth control pills are not a new form of Vitamin C, *believing* gets a bit more difficult.

The pre-teenager and teenager, equipped with an active hormonal system, tends to become deeply suspicious of Mommy's 3:00 a.m. returns home, with petticoat inside out, hair askew, and nylons tucked in her purse. Sooner or later, depending on their degree of aggressiveness, they will eventually ask if you are doing anything with Rodney, or as a friend's daughter bluntly put it, "Did you ever touch his wienie?"

Such queries, deserve only one answer, "None of your business." State it flat and outright. If you try, as I initially did, to say something diddly—like, "When people fall in love, there are many things they want to share,"—be prepared for such questions as "Does he stick it up your butthole?" and "You didn't taste it, did you?"

There are those folk who believe in being perfectly up front with their offspring, explaining personal activities in common or scientific language, but generally speaking "None of your business" works better. And if the inquisition continues, try "Ask me again when you're 30, and I'll be glad to answer."

Evading explanations of your own personal doings is not an excuse for children not knowing the facts of life. They should, and early, too. Otherwise, all the information they get comes from television talk shows, giving a rather unbalanced perspective on the complexities of relationships. Clip out the Ann Landers columns if you have to, and read them aloud. Post informational items on the refrigerator, if you're really embarrassed. Knowledge goes a long way in today's risky climate.

In the meantime, how much do the children get involved with Rodney? This seems to vary with each parent. Some of my friends make it a point to involve their steady dates with their offspring. They go to plays or bowling together, or have regular fireside chats. No particular harm seems to come from this, except the kids can get pretty attached to Rodney. When this happens, they also become somewhat upset when he leaves and another fine fellow takes his place.

Frankly, I have a marked preference for keeping *my* social life *mine.* Just as I do not tag along with the younger set when they go fishing, roller skating, or to the ice cream parlor, I seldom involve the youngsters with my social life. My guy doesn't have to pretend to enjoy the nit-picking quibbles which go on between my quibbly daughters, nor do I have to spend the entire time pretending to be Mother of the Year, all the while glaring at my kids when Rodney's back is turned.

Of course, if I ever met someone with whom I seriously contemplated a permanent life-sharing arrangement, things would be different. Then the children would accompany us often. I would want to see how the fellow related to them during stress periods—his and theirs.

More subsequent marriages break up because of the children than any other factor. So the social statistic keepers say, and so say my friends who have been there. You cannot assume, because you're happy, the kids won't make you unhappy. They may not like a parent replacement threat. So test a lot of the waters first.

The Dating Teenager and Dating Mommy

There is a very unexpected and full blown guilt trip that comes about when your teenager starts dating and Mommy starts re-dating. If you come from a traditional house, where Mom puts on a housedress and fuzzy slippers, then paces the floor waiting for Junior to return, you have a lot of upside down adjusting to do.

If you have daughters, you may find yourself turning down dates so you can pace the floor until Priscilla returns. You also feel you have to be home to meet Priscilla's beau, you must be near a telephone in case there are any problems, and you have to be home to make certain she gets home safely.

If you have sons, worries tend to be different. You worry whether Percy has cracked up the family car, again, and that's why he's 55 minutes later than the promised 2:00 a.m. You worry whether he will get some unworthy girl pregnant. You worry whether he mouthed off at somebody, and got his teeth knocked out.

All this worry, whether Percy or Priscilla, can ruin your own social life. After all, it's hard to get a teenage babysitter to babysit your teenager while you go out and have a good time.

The first time my daughter goes out with Prince Charming, I make every effort to stay home. He's probably fine, but he may turn out to be Prince Chugalugging. If I can't stay home the entire time, I leave after my daughter leaves, and try my best to get home before she's expected home. If her first date turns out fine with the fellow, the next time our social lives coincide, I leave her a number, as usual, where I can be reached.

It never gets much easier. I still say a small prayer when I am gone at the same time my daughter is out on a date. But if you abandon your social life until the children are 22, 42, or 62, then you will become a hovering, overprotective nag with no life outside of work and the kitchen walls. And your children will not appreciate this. Quite the contrary, they have a tendency to turn around and smack the single parent right in the solar plexus with, "Well, nobody told you to," "Isn't it about time you tried to make a life of your own and stop hanging onto mine," and "Mother, get off my back."

This will wound you to the core. You will begin resenting everything you gave up. Some things in life get easier as one gets older. Resuming an active social life after staying home is seldom one of these. You get somewhat set in your ways, and also more timid. It's best to try and achieve some balance between your child's social life and your own. You may have to force yourself out of the fuzzy slipper routine at first, but you will get used to it after a while and it won't seem quite so devastating.

Horizons are still not entirely clear; there's another built in guilt trip on the single mother's scene. If you have a beau and Junior does not, you may feel terrible as you get dressed up in frilly finery for an evening out. Junior will stare at you in the most woebegone fashion, trying to figure out what's wrong with him/her if an *old lady* can attract the opposite sex, but Junior can't seem to.

Under such circumstances, it may be hard to ask your wistful dateless child how you look, but you also don't want to get dressed in a closet and crawl out the attic window. Besides, this sets a bad example for the next generation. So make a special attempt to talk about your upcoming evening, and get Junior's input whenever possible. Junior is probably much more up-to-date on current cultural events than you are, so ask for movie suggestions and places to go for ice cream afterward. If you have daughters, you might also consult with them on appropriate attire for the evening.

With my daughters, just like my mother used to, they want my hemlines lower, my necklines higher, my make-up minimal, and my attitude puritan. If I'm trying to figure out whether my escort is of the handholding species or the lunge-grapple species, I chat about that casually, too. Sometimes I actively seek out Junior's opinion on how to handle questions of who pays for what and when, that type of thing. Sometimes Junior and I get philosophical, as we discuss whether I am going out for the evening because my date is a person, or because he is a *date.*

It makes no difference whether Junior is experienced or a total novice on the male-female social scene. Kids like to be asked for advice. They are likely to be more clearheaded than adults in their thinking, too.

Even that novice child of yours may have dating friends, or friends with older siblings making the romance scene. They may have sat in on multiple rap sessions. Comments on coping methods, albeit secondhand, can be very helpful. You may have known it all one Cinderella time, but you don't know the rules, if there are any, in this modern day and age. You are in for marked re-entry culture shock if you were married more than five years ago, or have moved from Big Apple to Little Peach, or vice-versa.

If Junior has something to say, listen. You will not only learn valuable tidbits about current trends, but also a great deal about the child you are raising to be an intelligent human being. And be sure to thank Junior for his/her help, whether you intend to use it or not. This gives Junior a sense of importance, and of being an integral part of your team.

If you appreciate your child's support, good wishes will follow you out the door instead of jealousy. And if, while saying thank you, you tell Junior the help will be reciprocated when she/he has a beau/girlfriend, you are making an implied promise of a rosier future. Children have faith that Mother knows about such things. Your reward can be a smile which says Junior can wait a little longer for a date. This goes a long way toward making your guilt trip a very short excursion.

However, your job isn't over yet. The next item on your agenda is anecdote sharing. This should come the day after your evening social expedition. For example, if Chock-Full-Of-Looks turned out to have the conversational ability of clam chowder, say so. "He wouldn't say anything, and I spent the entire evening babbling like an idiot to prevent endless silence."

Such commentary will actually help immensely when Junior goes out with a personal clam jaws and tends to feel at fault for a bad social encounter. Someplace in the back of her/his brain will be the remembrance of Mom's fiasco. And if this can happen to Mom, who can hold a conversation with almost everybody, then Junior isn't being singled out for punishment. This can help a tender ego and prevent teenage depression, another modern phenomenon.

You might also share the tale of the date who drinks too much and wants to get you equally sloshed in hopes the alcohol will make you fervently romantic. I had one date, Henry, who started thinking I had a cast iron stomach. He persisted in ordering scotch and sodas for me, rather than letting me nurse my usual single shot until the ice melted. So I merely waited until he almost finished his drink, then kept switching glasses when his back was turned. He staggered out of the cocktail lounge, amazed at my capacity. He also didn't have the strength left to protest when I insisted on driving home.

Hopefully, your child may not come across this particular situation until he/she is of legal drinking age. Still, you have sent the message that they don't have to let a tanked date get behind the wheel. Let them know that if a problem ever occurs, you'll be glad to pick Junior up, or that taxi fare will be reimbursed.

You should also casually mention that in a party situation, when being part of the crowd is also part of the party, Seven-Up on ice with a twist of lime looks quite like a martini, or somesuch. An alternative (one I successfully used as a teen) is taking the drink an ever-hopeful date sticks in your hand, taking a sip, then forgetting the glass on a corner table.

You can never assume, whatever their age, that spirits will be unavailable to your child. Even at the safest appearing parties, some yo-yo may sneak in a bottle of hootch, or pour one into the punch bowl. Nagging on this subject tends to plug a child's ears, but if you tell what happened to you, and what you did about it, that's a story, not a nag. Since kids love stories, the message tends to get through more readily.

Approaching such serious topics somewhat sideways also encourages the kids to tell you stories, too. That lets you know what their friends are up to, permitting Mom to come up with appropriate blocking mechanisms when necessary.

As a single parent, you are luckier on this issue than a half-of-a-pair parent. When you talk of your experiences on the modern social scene, nobody grunts and says, "But Mom, that all happened centuries ago." Your experiences are current. They happened as recently as last night. Some are admittedly funny. Most have a subtle moral message. They're all great conversational items at the dinner table, and by far beat "What did you do at school today?"

Can you feel guilty when Junior laughs at Romeo's antics? Isn't it fun when Junior actually begins looking forward to Mom's evening out with a new beau? Anecdote sharing tends to be a great envy douser. Try it a few times. You'll be amazed at the results. You may even be asked to repeat stories when teenage friends visit, thus expanding everybody's horizons, including yours.

Daughter's Got a Boyfriend—You Don't

Sometimes, perhaps oftentimes, you don't have a beau. Cold showers aren't working. You're climbing the walls. There is this intense feeling that if somebody doesn't come along and hold your hand, you are going to scream.

Given the vagaries of chance, this set of miseries can be accompanied by Priscilla wandering in with Mr. Super Gorgeous. Now it's your turn for those flickers of envy starting at your toes and gnawing at your innards.

Before you realize what you're doing, you are wearing your hair just a bit curlier, putting on that nice clinging dress, and slipping into quite high heels. All this is done in subconscious anticipation that Mr. Super Gorgeous will look your way and give a flicker of approval.

It's all perfectly straightforward, of course. You want to look nice for your child's new friend. You want to be hospitable. That's why you keep interrupting their conversation with offers of cookies and hot chocolate. It's why you join in the conversation. You want the young man to feel comfortable.

A married woman playing this silly game might be able to wing it, courtesy of her wifely status. But you aren't married anymore, so you can't get away with it. Instead, try cold showers, or jogging. Leave Mr. Super Gorgeous alone despite your current beau-less condition.

You are entitled to be in the house, and should be, when your daughter entertains male company. You are not entitled to be in the same room, unless there's only one room in the house. Hot chocolate and cookies are fine, but let your teenager do the serving. Your activities are limited to turning on the tea kettle. Your nice dress is also fine, but it's quite proper of you to try and look a bit motherly. If you only own slinky attire, wear it with sneakers and bobby socks. It helps.

Keeping out of the conversation, except for opening pleasant-ries, is more difficult. It's so easy to justify casual conversation as harmless. Yet you can just as easily work off your need to talk by giving a call to 90-year-old Aunt Elsie or Uncle Louis, both of whom would truly appreciate hearing from anybody. Not only will you be doing a good deed, you will be setting a good example, which is what parenting is all about.

Sons and Dating Mothers

It is definitely much harder, in many ways, to bring up sons without a father than it is to bring up daughters without a father. Some erst- while sociologist has actually demonstrated that women with male children tend to stay married longer than women with female children. Realizing that little boys often need big boys as role models, you may have persisted with Eclipse just so Junior could watch somebody shave their face in the morning rather than their legs.

But now that Junior is shaving (or nearly so), you start looking around for surrogates to pick up the slack. If you are lucky, there's a nearby cousin, uncle, or grandfather who visits, or is visited, often enough to provide a solid masculine image.

If you are not so lucky, you haul Junior around to assorted Scout troops, baseball groups, and soccer clubs. There's always the hope that coaches or other daddy-types will provide enough visual bits and pieces that Junior gets the idea.

Good enough, yet not good enough. Many single mothers want more personal attention given to their sons. This is one reason to bring gruff- voiced, denim-clad males through your castle door.

Yet, contrary to expectations, Junior hates the visitor on sight, and before sight. He sulks, throws temper tantrums, or hides in his room and won't come out. "I've already got a daddy," Junior says, "and nobody's going to take his place." He's likely also thinking, "I can take care of you. Why do you need anybody else?"

You plead, cajole and bribe. Eventually Junior emerges. Instead of trying to be friendly, he glares at the intruder during the entire afternoon or evening. But, despite this, your date may be willing to make conversational efforts. Junior grunts single-syllable responses and stares at his ankles.

Your date begins to get a bit sullen. He perhaps suggests that Junior must have had some bad experiences with your other male friends. Your date also figures he came for a pleasant afternoon. The next time he does it, the afternoon will be with someone else. If Junior stays wide awake and watchdog until 2:00 a.m., your beau learns to avoid nice ladies with not-nice kids.

However you may hit it lucky and find a beau that remembers what it's like to be a little boy, or likes you enough to work harder at being nice to Junior. You maneuver it so big boy and little boy play tag football on the lawn. The three of you share hot dogs at a professional ball game. Big boy even helps little boy dig for fishing worms, and he takes a stab at helping with the home- work.

Junior is now looking forward to your beau's visits. He even starts thinking in terms of having two daddies. One daddy visits occasionally, the other will truly live with him. He will even have somebody to take to Father-Son Day at school, just like the other kids.

You are beginning to think your problems are over. Except one evening you and beau decide you're not for each other. The next morning you get to explain this to Junior. Regardless of what you say, Junior begins thinking, "Another daddy has left me. What am I doing wrong?"

You understand. You sympathize. You don't want your child to be hurt again. Yet you can't stop dating until Junior takes off with the Air Force.

More male friends visit your castle. In time, Junior stops getting hurt by their disappearance and, instead, he emotionally turns off on all your beaus. He begins viewing them as an endless procession of masculine bodies coming through the door and eventually leaving.

It is not likely to get any easier as Junior gets older. "Teenage boys have this *thing* about their mothers," my friend Diane comments. "Their sexuality is in full swing. They're quite aware of what can happen between males and females. Frankly, I think my son would like to buy me a chastity belt, and have me wear it 24 hours a day. I'm supposed to be a madonna, or something."

The older Junior gets, the more knowledge he acquires from television, movies, his friends, and the back seat of cars. Sometimes you are tempted to quit dating, just to make peace. Other times you persist in dating, and try to cope. All this comes at a time when you are feeling increasingly powerless at dealing with normal teen-age independence.

Consider doing what growing numbers of single mothers today do; turn Junior over to his father. Junior may request this transfer, even if you don't want it. You are more likely to be faced with one of these options if you have a live-in beau, or you remarry. In these situations, each male, Junior and New Husband/Guy, likes to rule his own roost. There is a natural conflict over pecking order.

Most often, you and Junior just hang in there. It may be for lack of alternatives, or because you really love each other despite occasionally hating each other. Many wonderful, honorable men have been raised by single mothers. Those who have a caring mother who put her parental role first turn out to be hard-working gentlemen with a deep respect for Mother, as well as other women.

Recent statistics suggest that mothers who only have boys tend to stay married longer than mothers who only have girls. It is indeed a job to watch Junior grow from his first toddling steps into a self-sufficient mature adult. But, if you hang in there, you can accomplish that goal, despite the obstacles.

Little Feet Round-Up

Sometimes, as a single mother, you wonder what happened to *you*. You get the patter of little feet, while Daddy gets all the freedom. You get to take ice-cold showers, Daddy has live-in lovers. Many's the time you figure there's no justice in the world. You are tempted to pack up the old kit bag, turn little patter feet over to whomever will have them, and just travel the open road.

But, as valid as these frustrations are, there are real joys to your lot in life. Kids are truly nice people (especially when they're sleeping). If you have a hard day at work, you can come home and peek at their angel faces snuggled against the crumpled pillow.

If you do it right, raising kids is like money in the bank. You may have to omit the fancy dinner and sequined hosiery to come up with the necessary dimes and quarters. But in the long run, you've packed away a nice savings account of love for the future.

What difference does it make if you lose a beau or two by not letting him sleep in Daddy's bed? The men I've met with respect for my home as a home, also have great respect for a woman keeping it that way. That's the type of guy you want anyhow. While there's a certain percentage that panic because of the kids, there's another fair-sized percentage that likes kids. Kids keep them youthful, and they know it.

Single mothers who manage to raise their children alone, do without a lot of things and put up with a lot of things. They are also mighty proud of themselves for surviving, and succeeding.

It's a pride quite different from that of a mother in a two-parent family. It's hard to explain, but maybe you know what I mean. It's that feeling of, "I did it myself. I didn't think I could. But I did. And I did a pretty good job."

In the long run, there's something extremely satisfying about doing a pretty good job, no matter what it takes.

SOLO PARENT,
WILL TRAVEL

If, over the course of your marriage, solo excursions have been limited to local supermarket shopping sprees, singledom is a brand new game. You may begin it huddled on the front stoop, enviously watching paired neighbors taking off on their glorious vacations.

Confronted with the instant realization that Daddy did almost all of the long-haul driving, you may think you are stuck at home forever. Alternatives appear to be (1) finding a masculine re-placement willing to drive several bright-eyed, noisy youngsters to anyplace; (2) taking a walk around the block to visit your former mother-in-law; (3) encouraging your children to synchronize their whines of "our friends are all away and we have nothing to do," and trying to peddle it as a hit tune.

Terror makes a prison as much as bars. Once upon a time, I too used to break out in a cold sweat at the mere thought of placing four feisty kids in a car and taking them anyplace. But, eventually, enough was enough. Mommy made her first attempt to leave her cell block, and discovered it wasn't so traumatic after all—once she learned the ropes.

Over the years, the children and I have explored neighboring cities, gone camping, visited resorts, and even traveled cross-country via train. Considering my youngest was only 4 months old when these excursions began, sometimes I wondered if there was a danger of dislocating my shoulder from patting myself on the back. Perhaps, you want to try it too?

Saturday Is Fun Day

To gain confidence, start with excursions within an hour's drive. Most newspapers have a weekly listing of local activities. Many of these are free, or of minimal cost.

There are three basic rules for choosing an outing: (1) the children should enjoy the activity; (2) you should not have to say "Shhh" at whatever place you are going; (3) there has to be run-around space.

Since this is your fun day, too, you don't want to spend it nagging and chasing. You want to share ideas and the spirit of adventure. That way the kids, as well as their solo parent, eagerly ask when they can go again?

Here is a list of my favorite local destinations. You can certainly add to this, or change it, depending on where you live and what your family prefers.

1. All-breed dog shows
2. Doll and miniature exhibitions
3. Folk dance festivals
4. Guided nature walks
5. Military base open houses
6. Kite flying contests
7. Sand castle contests
8. Collections of vintage planes or autos
9. Rock and mineral shows
10. Any natural science center with plenty of snakes and spiders

Be aware that carnivals are very expensive, and they can make it hard to keep an eye on the kids. Zoos are okay, if the children enjoy the animals, and not just the cotton candy.

Museums, I have learned the hard way, are places to avoid. You have to keep the kids too quiet, and watch them constantly so they don't poke anything antique or priceless. One exception to this general rule is a really great fossil or mummy exhibit. Kids really enjoy life-sized skeletons of scary dinosaurs, and the sight of neatly bandaged King Tut provides better thrills than a late-night rerun of *Frankenstein's Uncle*. Another nice thing about mummies and dinosaurs is they're usually locked up behind bars or glass, so the kids don't have to cope with the museum guard.

If you are fortunate enough to live near a children's museum, this is another notable exception. Here, the kids are encouraged to touch and feel the exhibits and discover what makes them special. These rare finds can be real learning experiences for both the kids and you.

I do, however, make a cultural foray into art museums once in a while. The children's commentary on Picasso, Renoir, and the modernists borders on the unprintable. So, Mommy has devised a little game, which somewhat eases her suffering and may help you.

Each child is told to walk around and pick out a favorite picture in each room. They report the winner to me, and tell me why it was selected. This not only gives you a few minutes peace and quiet to enjoy the art work, but often provides you with amazing insights into each child's perception of beauty.

What the heck, it's worth a try at least. If it doesn't work, you can always go outside and feed the seagulls your leftover hot dogs.

While on the topic of hot dogs, remember that they're no longer cheap fodder. Part of your excursion preparation should be sack lunches. Peanut butter and jelly is just fine. You won't cry if the leftovers are fed to the birds. Accompany sandwiches with the children's favorite cookies and tab-open fruit punch, plus plenty of paper napkins.

If you have a baby, leave the balanced-diet-in-a-jar at home for the day. Bring along pre-mixed formula in individual, easy-open cans. For solid food, bring along zwieback or vanilla wafers, which the baby can suck on. If you want more protein, sliced American cheese works well.

If Baby is a wee infant, or if a toddler isn't potty trained, don't forget the extra diapers. Ecologically, paper diapers are a no-no, but they are great for traveling. To tote Baby, forget that plastic infant seat. It only seems light weight for the first one-eighth of a mile. After that even a preemie seems to gain a pound a minute. Instead, take a fold-up, portable, one-hand-push, extremely light-weight stroller. Not only will the ruts in the road help rock the baby to sleep, but your older children can help you push.

Portable strollers are such wonderful aids, that I brought mine along until my youngest was 5 years old. I would have used it even longer, but she refused, saying, "I'm bigger now."

Yet, even if you have the best of food and equipment, neglecting the time factor quickly turns Fun Day into a disaster. Endurance time for pre-teen youngsters is a maximum of 4 hours, including travel time.

Leave the house as early as possible in the morning, but try to avoid the early morning commuter traffic. You want the kids to be wide awake, and Mommy not yet tuckered out from household chores.

If you get lost on the way, you can ruin your trip. Call your destination before you leaven, and get detailed driving directions. Double check the directions against a map, because people tell you left turn when it should be right turn, and street signs can be hidden behind trees.

Bring a map along just in case. Don't rely on a gas station to have maps these days, nor on station employees for appropriate help. Station turnover is high, employees may be new to the area, and they don't always speak English.

Inquire about parking beforehand, and on arrival head directly for your planned activity. Don't get sidetracked into spending just-a-few-minutes at something else. Resist the temptation to get interested in the antique furniture displays. The nervous twitches you save may be your own.

As the day progresses, the children may appear to have boundless energy. You may begin to feel cocky about their staying power. So you get the urge to make a whole day of it. Forget it!

Happy children can turn into warthogs in the blink of an eye. Go while the going's good and beat rush hour traffic. You can always come back another time. If you play your planning-cards right, that's exactly what Mommy and Junior will want to do.

Hooray for Holidays

As your confidence gradually increases, you will stop envying your neighbor's vacations and start planning your own. Before you begin pouring over exotic travel brochures, try local, overnight travel. It's a whole different ball game when Mommy is solo captain of the ship and there's no Daddy to help bail out the leaks.

Where can you go? My first weekend excursion was a YMCA family camp. We had comfortable cabins, bunk beds, prepared meals, and counselor led activities. There were adults to keep me company, kids to keep my kids company, and ample supervision. In addition, the cost was quite reasonable.

Universities have family camps which are not limited to students. Call their recreation association and ask for information. Church groups sponsor family excursions, as do some city park districts. Single's groups, such as Parents Without Partners, also have family outdoor activity.

What should you bring, in addition to mosquito repellent? Whatever it is, keep it light. Again, Daddy is not along to tote the heavy stuff. I learned my lesson after one session of dragging suitcases uphill to a tent. Sometimes on a camping excursion you can't park near where you're sleeping, and even with single's groups you can't count on male help.

All clothing must be in dirt defying colors, and made of drip dry fabric. A modern advantage, should everything you own become covered with mud, is that most places within sight of civilization have a coin laundromat. Otherwise, you can wash everything in the bathroom sink, and throw together a makeshift clothes line.

To avoid squabbles when one sibling is searching for a purple sock and instead latches onto older siblings purple underwear, use plastic or paper garbage bags as individual wardrobe containers. These same reusable, plastic garbage bags, available in many sizes, can be used for a multitude of purposes. In go wet towels, soggy bathing suits, transit food supplies, along-the-road rock collections, or messy diapers.

If you are traveling with an infant, a half dozen cloth diapers should augment the convenient disposables. in case you run out of disposables, and midnight supermarkets aren't available. Baby's attire, demanding quick access, is best placed in a separate duffle-bag.

In addition to the pre-mixed formula and throwaway type bottles, always include a blanket sleeper and a warm knitted cap—

even in summer. The weatherperson isn't always right, and temperatures anyplace tend to drop at night. And remember, excursions are a lot more fun when you take the baby out to the campfire and marshmallow roast.

Once you have discovered the pleasures of solo-parent overnights with kids, you will be eager to attempt longer voyages. My first longer voyage was another *safe* trip, this time to a family camp run by the city and located in a national park. This was a marvelous sharing experience with the children. I also learned quite a bit, making future trips much easier.

The first thing learned was to always carry a supply of carsick pills. These are available without prescription at most pharmacies. The second essential task was to dose up the child who always got carsick before the trip. Once a tummy gets woozy, a child generally can't swallow anything.

I learned this valuable lesson one day, as I attempted to negotiate a very winding stretch of uphill road. I was terrified, because I hate uphill curves, particularly in 90 degree weather when my car threatens to overheat.

This was the stretch of road where my dear child decided to barf consistently. My ample supply of easily accessible bath towels and garbage bags came in very handy. Every single one was utilized in just a half-hour. When we finally got a chance to rest, I strapped all the aromatic bags to the car roof. Eventually, we arrived safely in camp—barf bags and all.

With the kids around as conversational ice breakers, it's easy to forget your troubles. At family camps there are two parent, one parent, and miscellaneous parent families, and even solos who attend because they like the protected atmosphere. You can talk if you choose, but you're not obligated. If you think the squirrels are a bit more stimulating than the other campers, that's okay, too. One definite advantage of single parent traveling is you don't have to be social unless it's something you want.

Of course, if you travel in spring and summer, you will soon be socializing with mosquitoes. They appear in the morning, and remain attached to everybody until the moon ices over. My youngsters complained loudly about this when I neglected to bring mosquito repellent and we found the camp store closed. I had to think quickly, so I ended their gripes by promising a candy bar to the child with the most red welts at day's close.

This brings us to the subject of that all important medical kit. In it goes ointment for bites, baby and adult aspirin or non-aspirin pain reliever, thermometer, bandages, tweezers, emery boards, adhesive tape, allergy pills, cough syrup, and a mild over the counter antibiotic cream.

Chances are you won't need any of this, but should stuffy nose, splinters, or tumbles threaten to mar your good times, it helps to have it close at hand. In addition, make certain you and the children are up to date with your tetanus shots.

A few other items which it helps to have tucked away someplace include small scissors, several sewing needles, thread, small plastic bottles of shampoo and washing detergent, and several flashlights with fresh batteries.

Even if you aren't going camping, flashlights come in handy. Youngsters who wake up in a strange room often want to know where Mommy is. I carry one flashlight for each of my children to sleep with.

Far Away Begins to Look Easier

Once the minutiae becomes automatic, you can expand your solo parent destinations. Start thinking of days on the road, rather than hours. The world has now become your oyster. Go to the library and check out current travel books. Try writing to the National Park Service in Washington, DC for maps and guides. Send a note to the chamber of commerce in your target cities.

Start making plans at least a month in advance. Reservations may not have been high on the list when you were a two parent family, but they're extremely important when you are a solo parent. It is truly the pits to be exhausted from driving and find *No Vacancy* signs in every motel window except the one charging $100 a night.

If you can manage it, get an American Automobile Association (AAA) guidebook to the state you are visiting. It lists information about area lodgings, and scenic attractions on-route. There are other organizations, some run by the same folks who offer gas credit cards, which offer somewhat similar information. The best thing about these aids, besides the rate list, is that the places have been previewed for you, so you don't end up paying for some dive.

When looking up lodging in a guidebook, check first for a general price range, then zero in. Note whether a family plan is offered, where children under a certain age, usually twelve or sixteen, stay free with an adult. For the solo parent, this is quite a boon; I pay for myself, and my four kids room free.

You will also want a coffee shop on the premises or nearby, and a swimming pool during warm months. Mother usually needs a fresh cup of java to help her recuperate, and the children definitely need a place to work off steam after being confined to a car.

While you can make reservations through a travel club, I prefer to do my own by telephone. That way I get exactly what I want. For example, I prefer a room on the first floor, as close to the pool as possible. I dislike hauling luggage, like easy access to lobby candy machines and ice makers, and want to avoid such kiddy misadventures as the unauthorized use of strange elevators, running up and down stairways, or having an excuse to cruise the hallways.

If you need a room with a crib, most hotels and motels provide them at a minor extra charge. But since cribs might be in limited supply, do inquire about this when you reserve. If you need any rollaway beds, ask about those, too.

Get a firm price for everything. It's best to get a confirmation. This is easily done by writing a detailed note, and enclosing a self-addressed postcard for reply. It may seem a nuisance, but many lodgings routinely overbook, especially during holidays. This way, when they claim to have no record of your reservation, you can present the front desk with your written postcard confirmation.

While you're taking advance precautions, get your car checked out and repaired by a competent mechanic several weeks before you depart. Make it a special point to have your tires checked, including the spare, and replace tires as necessary.

One of every single mother's greatest fears is driving over unfamiliar terrain in a car threatening to break down at any moment. Generally, Murphy's Law provides that your lemon-auto will go kerplunk (1) in a town with a population of twelve, (2) on a Sunday when all service stations are bolted shut, and (3) when the weatherperson's predictions of 100 degree heat, or continuing downpour, have proved absolutely correct.

Never, even with a good car, drive after dark with children if you can avoid doing so. If you absolutely must, keep emergency flashers, food, water, and blankets in the car. Oh yes, and don't forget to have change for the telephone.

Once I thought there was nothing I could do about the nightmare that my old clunker would drop dead on an unfamiliar highway. I was conditioned to believe that ladies know nothing about cars, and working on them wasn't cute. It wasn't until I got ripped off for the umpteenth time by a mechanic who learned his trade at the slaughterhouse that I changed all that.

For a minimal fee, I enrolled in a basic auto repair course given two evenings a week at a local high school. There are similar offerings through community colleges, adult education services, and some auto clubs. I learned how to change a flat tire, how to check oil, water, and transmission fluids, and something about car sputters. (Some sputters are serious, others are merely warning signals.)

After the course, mechanical terminology, which once seemed to require a translator, now looked almost basic. And if you want to know the most common scams, a competent repair teacher can give you an earful, which will save you lots of bucks.

For example, one afternoon my car's turn signals stopped working. I pulled up at a service station where the attendant said my electrical system was in process of collapsing, and I should leave the car there, or else. They would call me when the required parts arrived. The estimated cost was a minimum of $150.

Having just completed the repair course, I rejected his appraisal and used hand signals the rest of the way home, where I replaced the car fuses for $2. That took care of the problem, and I didn't even get my hands dirty.

The following basic equipment should be carried in your car: Phillips screwdriver, standard screwdriver, powerful flashlight, cheapie flashlight, road flares, distilled water, tire jack, extra can of oil, at least one set of fuses, and jumper cables.

Once your mind has been set at ease regarding car breakdowns, the open road for the single mother looks less like an obstacle course. You can then turn your attention to keeping the children occupied while you zip along the roadways.

Road Games and Munchies

Games are part of any solo parent outing. Yet when Mother has her hands on the wheel, and her eyes riveted on the crazy drivers ahead and to the side, she can't exactly participate in Nintendo. Although you can play "A my name is Alice, I live in Argentina, and I eat apples," at least once, it gets old quickly, as do the endless rounds of "Row, Row, Row Your Boat." So children must learn to amuse themselves at least part of the time.

The best investment you can make on a car trip is two decks of playing cards. If you have three children, get three decks; this prevents quibbling. Some parents augment the toy box with crayons, coloring books, paper dolls, etc., but I find that little bits of paper make lots of mess, and children have a tendency to try throwing them out the window.

Personally, I use dimes and assorted other bribes to maintain some semblence of quiet, but no technique will prevent young squirmers from eventually asking, "When are we going to get there?" You can ease the aggravation this causes by employing several other maneuvers.

First, always give the kids a definite stopping time for the next rest break. It can be 3:00 p.m., or when you reach Ice Cream Junction. If you give them a time, hand them a cheap watch or small clock and let them pace the hours. If you give them a place, mark the location on a map and hand it to a child who can read.

When you come to the appointed time or place, you absolutely must keep your word and stop. Child travelers really do behave better if they know there's a reliable end to their confinement.

A basic gauge for pit stops should allow a 15 minute fresh air romp and potty stop for every 1½ driving hours. Keeping safety always in mind, stop at marked rest areas during the day (never at night), gas stations, or restaurant parking lots.

I once thought it would be terribly exciting to find a remote off-road scenic view as a temporary halting place. That was before

I tried it one late afternoon. In no time at all, I was the object of attention from a group of teenage boys who had nothing better to do then pull up in their hot rods and stare at the stupid tourists. So now I stick to populated areas.

Even if you must stop at concrete or barren dirt lots around a restaurant or rest stop, there is still plenty for the kids to do. For example, they can study ants. Find an ant hill or ant hole. Sprinkle a few cookie crumbs or potato chips as bait. Then have the kids guess how many tiny insects it takes to haul a big crumb down into the nest.

During this, you can point out how the ants all work together to get the job done, and how, therefore, they can all work together to make your trip a success. Even if they don't get the message, they will enjoy the ant show, and likely wish they could stay longer.

For more active rest stop games, be sure to pack a beach ball or tennis ball for the children to throw, or smash, about the area. You can also run races—Mommy against the kids. This unkinks your knees and actually makes you feel better, although it may not seem like it at the time.

You might also carry a compact bird identification book for the area you are traveling in, and try bird watching. These guides are available from libraries, or are really inexpensive to buy. If you see a bird, have the kids look it up and tell you what it is. They soon learn identifying characteristics, and it keeps them happy in the car or at a pit stop.

Another fun occupation is opening "Mother's Memory Bank." Children always love to hear stories about when they were little. A child's first words, their reaction to a new sibling, their artistic wallpaper creations, all are grist for your story mill.

My stories include recollections of one child taking my engagement ring to school and passing it around for Show and Tell, another taking her first solo walk behind the big garbage truck, etc. Sometimes I even tell them how they acted in my stomach. They can hear that over and over again.

For a change of pace, try "When Mommy Was Little." I talk about my grammar school, my first kiss (ugh!), and the boy I had a crush on who never noticed me. This is communication with a capital "C," and my offspring-audience hangs on every word.

Should you recall any stories that Grandma or Grandpa told about their childhood, that's an added bonus—plus a history lesson. Don't worry about repeating yourself. Kids can listen to this type of anecdote a zillion times and still ask for more.

After you tell some stories, the kids probably will start chiming in with things about their younger days that you have forgotten, or would like to forget. "I remember this really neat mudhole near the apartment. I baked you the biggest cake, Mommy, do you remember? It had frosting, too. When I brought it in the kitchen while you were mopping the floor, you got the funniest look on your face. But your were smiling, weren't you?"

Each story brings up another memory. The bubble gum incident. The soapsuds eating encounter. What the doctor said when you visited the emergency room. As long as your voice holds, the kids will listen forever.

By 4:00 p.m. you absolutely must stop for the night, and 3:00 p.m. is even better. You must give the children time to run about and swim—and Mommy, too.

Next, it's chow time. I permit one eat-out meal per traveling day. Other meals are crackers, cheese, fruit, and container juice. These are all purchased either before I leave, or at supermarkets along the way.

When it comes to restaurants in unfamiliar terrain, I learned the hard way to avoid them. In your home town, you pretty much know where the atmosphere is pleasant, service good, prices reasonable, and food edible. You also know which places are okay to bring young people.

In a strange town you may find slopped coffee, indifferent waitpersons, and burnt hamburgers at burning prices. You spend good money on poor eating. You're already tired, the kids are restless, and that can add up to chaos in a strange place. So, for eating out while traveling, I think the fast food chains win hands down. The prices are reasonable, you know what you're getting, and, best of all, you can sit at one table and the kids at another.

For breakfast, put a small container of milk in the motel room sink surrounded by ice, or in a small styrofoam cooler from home. Either way, the milk should still be cold in the morning. Serve it on those little assorted boxes of cereals, and you have a meal.

You'll also want to carry along a portable water boiler, either one of those metal dip things or a small electric pot. Motels used to have these items, but many don't anymore. They are useful for making hot chocolate, coffee, or those tidy ready-mix packets of instant hot cereal.

Add to the above a few bananas, plastic spoons, and throwaway cups, and you have a full course breakfast without leaving the motel room. Food at bedside also allows you to get on the road by 8:00 a.m., before the kids start feeling too frisky. And they can go back to sleep in the car, which is nice for Mommy.

A friend asked me to be sure and mention some travel games for older children. I like "Look at that lunatic." The only game piece you need is someone on the road who changes lanes without signaling.

The basic premise is that a person careless about one facet of auto safety will be equally careless everyplace else. The object of the game is to catch them in as many errors as possible: tailgating, speeding, passing on the curve, displaying an inability to drive in a straight line, weaving through traffic, and anything else tempting disaster.

Allow two points for each violation. Keep score, and encourage the children to comment on the possible consequences of each lunatic action. See if a highway patrolman emerges from behind a hill. If that happens, everybody in the car gives a rousing cheer, and the game has been won. To lose the game, the lunatic driver turns off before being caught. Then, everybody says, "There's never a cop around when you need one," and goes on to another car.

One consequence of this game is that the children become extremely aware of Mommy's driving habits. This will really keep you on your toes.

When you just can't stand the sound of children's chatter another minute, give each child a pack of sugarless gum. They will follow their natural tendencies and stuff several pieces in their mouths at once, and you can relish the sound of the snap, crackle, and pop. But at least they stop talking for a bit. This gives you time to hum a peaceful little tune.

You are on an adventure. You're off along the yellow brick road, and the city of Oz is just over the rainbow. All the voyages you take will become part of the memory book which your children will carry into adulthood. Each voyage leads to another sharing and learning experience.

Soon a new solo parent, huddled on the front stoop back home, says, "You're so brave to travel alone with kids." Nothing to it, you think. If you are prepared. Mention that you, too, were afraid once upon a time. Talk about all the places you've visited since then. Show slides. Then get out a map of America and start planning your next single-mother-with-children vacation.

SING A SONG OF SOLO

Picture yourself sending an engraved card to your ex-husband saying, "Thank you so much for tormenting me until I filed for divorce. I'll be forever grateful."

"Grateful for what?" you ask. Leaving you with a mountain of debts, children to raise unaided, memories of bitter battles, a pillow wet with endless tears, a self-image torn to shreds? Who wants to send a thank you card for that? You will.

Unless you enjoy carrying a grudge, time will take your emotions through varying stages. Initially, your urge to kill serves as a constant background to everything you do and say. This is followed by intermittent periods of disgust. Next comes intermittent dislike.

Emotions surge and ebb. A year goes by, then another. One afternoon Eclipse says or does something that only a while ago would have had you in conniption fits. Now you respond, "Good grief, is he at it again?"

You move on to an attitude of semi-tolerance. Some wise person once said that the opposite of love is not hate, it's indifference. And so, you reach the point where occasional thoughts of Eclipse cross your mind, then disappear, as do all fleeting images of the past. There are bridges you will move over, gradually, not recognizing where your steps are leading.

Then, one afternoon, an acquaintance will ask you about Eclipse's welfare. Eclipse who? After all, you know several persons of that name, can they be more specific. Oh, they're talking about your ex-husband. He's fine, you guess. You really don't care. Isn't that nice.

Once you have shed the heavy burden of past grudges, your step will be lighter. You are now free! Yes, you have a gaggle of kids, and an 8:00 to 5:00 job, and occasionally you have to dust while you cope with chaos. But you also are in charge of your own life. Sometimes it zigs when it should have zagged, but you can take care of that. You are quite capable. Self-assurance rests comfortably on your shoulders, along with your new responsibilities.

A door that slammed shut, maybe the day you married, maybe long before that when you first heard that getting a husband should be your ultimate goal in life, has now opened again. You are prepared to have a quite-satisfactory life as a single female in today's world.

Divorce, fortunately or unfortunately, is quite common. While there are still frowners, few families cast the first stone anymore. There are few families untouched by divorce, regardless of religion, social status, etc. Even those bastions of social consciousness, the conservative women's magazines, now have articles dealing with divorce and remarriage. They even have fiction dealing with single mothers. Wow! Not only do you have a tremendous support group out there, you have plenty of company.

Solo Parent Advantages

Let's suppose you want to take off and go beachcombing with the kids this weekend. If you had a husband, he might want to stay home and fix the truck. If he stayed home, he might insist you keep him company. Without this stricture, you pack peanut butter and jelly sandwiches, a beach blanket, and leave. No hassle.

You happen to enjoy eating crackers in bed, while reading a gothic novel until 2:00 a.m. While you're at it, you like to slather aloe vera cream all over your body as a night-time beauty treatment. If you are married, your spouse might say, "Get your crumbs off my side," and "Do you have to grease yourself up like a turkey?"

and "D__ it, turn off the light already." As a single person, eat, grease, and read away.

Come Sunday morning, with the kids engrossed in television cartoons, you can sleep until noon if you want to. When you arise, you can wander around the house in your ratty robe, or look out the window and admire the birds. Nobody disturbs your train of thought.

Should Myra invite you for a cup of coffee and a quart of gossip, you don't have to ask permission, you just scoot on over. If she telephones you about the latest poop, you can prop your feet up on a chair and stay there until almost forever. No husband's snippy comments interrupt you. Isn't that nice?

Along comes paycheck time. You've nickled and dimed toward college expenses, a new couch, or a vacation. Once upon a past, your husband might have insisted on spending that money on his new power saw. Now, if a power saw graces your garage, you bought it. You bought it because you have learned to use it, and you want it. You, the former Jane of all thumbs.

Come evening, you may have a genuine headache. You don't want to do anything. So you don't. The children really do like leftover chicken on hamburger buns. Particularly if they're hungry enough and that's what's in the refrigerator. You can crawl between rumpled sheets, read a book on beauty techniques, and fall asleep with it on your stomach. At 2:00 a.m., nobody tells you to roll over and enjoy. You get some real rest, and get rid of the headache.

Your time is your own. Days may be too long, or too short, but you have some control over them. There's no other mule tugging in the other direction.

Yet, you say, you *need* a man around. You may not say this as loudly, or as often, as you did when first singled, but you still whisper it once in a while when the moon is full, when you're feeling pretty, when you want a shoulder to slightly-cry on.

Okay, so let's look at the disadvantages of being single.

Hold Me, Kiss Me, Thrill Me

You take off and go beachcombing with the kids. Everybody else seems to have come in couples. You want an adult to listen to that seashell with you, but there isn't one. Beaches are places where the heart takes sail along with the boats on the horizon. So loneliness tugs at your soul, like wind at a schooner.

You eat crackers in bed. They go crunch, crunch, crunch in a silence filled only by the ticking of the clock. Aloe vera is fine to try and ward off wrinkles, but there's no one around who cares whether you have them or not. And when you come to the scary part in the novel, you want a fuzzy chest to hide your face in. Only there's no fuzz, and the only chest is a chest of drawers.

Come Sunday morning, you yawn and stretch. It is noon. There's nobody to cook a fancy brunch for, you haven't really planned the day, and when you go outside all the neighbors are gadding in twosies. So you go back inside.

When Myra invites you for a cup of coffee and conversation, you may not really be in the mood. You wish you had a convenient, polite excuse—like a husband. You don't mind being the one to tell the kids they, *"can't* ... not ever," but from time to time you truly would like a tenor or baritone voice to back you up by saying, "You listen to your Mother now."

Your paycheck arrives. You get a smidge of a raise in salary. It's nothing to crow about, but at least you would like a chance to cheep. Only a husband, sharing the bills, appreciates a smidge of a salary raise. A husband sees you every day and knows how hard you work at that job.

Evening falls and you actually have a genuine headache. You want somebody to massage your neck. Rubbing your own neck doesn't provide the same soothing effect. And sometimes you do wake up at 2:00 a.m. needing a bit of extra rubbing here and there. It's not the same when you do it yourself.

Yes, you can get temporary male replacements. When they get tired, you get tired, or everybody's space changes, you, he, or everybody can get up and go. You both pretend it's not as traumatic, because there's no official piece of paper to bind you, but it is traumatic. You shed tears just the same.

You want someone around permanently. Just to be there; nothing fancy. Still, you're not willing to jump into a rotten marriage again. So, with good men being hard to find, being single will just have to do. For the now, or for perhaps longer than that.

The Melody Changes

"I got married again after I had been single 15 years," says Christina, a very attractive brunette in her early fifties. "I just happened to meet a very nice man and figured I might as well take the plunge. Sometimes I feel like that plunge was from a warm shower into a cold one. You just don't realize how accustomed you get to doing things your own way.

"If you get married fairly young, as I did, before your personality forms, you share and adapt without thinking too much about it. Women are trained to adapt, trained to compromise. It's part of our heritage.

"Then you get singled. You get blasted out into the no job, no money, no street smarts scene. Somehow you manage to survive. Then you go one better. You learn to competently handle this and take charge of that. All the way you like to do it.

"Just when the path seems perfectly comfortable, you say 'I do' again. Suddenly everything flips topsy turvy. My husband likes the dishes in the dishwasher arranged just so. In retaliation, I re-arrange the tools he's got in the garage. He prefers a spick-and-span apartment. Frankly, I don't care if there's dust in every corner, and on table tops, besides. I'm a morning person. He grumps in the morning. I can't stand a grumpy person in the morning. He says the same thing about me in the evening.

"But we're trying. It seems to be getting better. The second time around, you either try harder or jump out faster. That's something you've learned along the way too."

Sometimes, Christina wishes she was single again. "It's a lot easier," she admits. "It's not so confining." Other times, she's glad to wake up with a known somebody beside her. Even if he snores.

"But I wouldn't have traded my independent years for anything in the world," she concludes. "I got the opportunity to grow, to become a self-sufficient person. I am now another person entirely. I could never have done this if I'd continued with my first marriage, even if it had been a good one. Being single today is a fantastic opportunity. There's no other way to look at it."

I asked Christina if she would ever consider thanking her former spouse. She mulled that over for a bit. "I might think about it," she said, "but I'd never do it."

It's just an idea, but wouldn't life be ever so much pleasanter if we could all shake hands, make warfare a distant memory, and declare a permanent truce?

You still can't see yourself approaching Eclipse and saying, "I'll be forever grateful?" Well, you'll change. One serene evening, when you've just succeeded at something else new and difficult, you'll think about it. And you may say "thank you," even if it's only a refrain running through your mind.

Thank you for helping me sing a solo song.